SPEAKER'S

SCRAPBOOK

Compiled by

Albert L. Zobell, Jr.

Bookcraft
Salt Lake City, Utah

Lithographed in the United States of America
PUBLISHERS PRESS
Salt Lake City, Utah

COMPILER'S PREFACE

Speaker's Scrapbook is another in the "Storyteller's Scrapbook" series.* We hope that it fills your need for this moment's inspirational thought as well as your preparation for your coming lesson presentations.

—Albert L. Zobell, Jr.

*Titles in the Series are: *Storyteller's Scrapbook, Storyettes, Story Gems, Story Sermons, Story Classics, Story Quotes, Story Lore, Story Beacons, Story Wisdom, Sermon Seedlings, Thoughts for Talks, Keys to Wisdom, Modern Parables, Quills of Truth, Topic Echoes, Notes to Quote, Talk Capsules, You, Too, Remember . . ., File Favorites,* and *Mini-Talks.* Earlier Bookcraft titles were: *Minute Sermons* and *Sunlight and Shadows.*

The Biblical Proverbs counsel:

"In all thy ways acknowledge him, and he shall direct thy paths."—Proverbs 3:6

CONTENTS

Contents

ACCOMPLISHMENT

We see all about us good starters but poor stayers. Many lives fail from inability to deliver the last blow. The ability to carry the last rampart, to fight to the end of the day, is the ability that conquers.

In baseball it may be important to get to third base, but this depends chiefly upon what one does when he gets there. Three-quarter runs are never marked up on the scoreboard. Third base is not a destination, but the last little way-station on the road home. If you die on third you are a failure. You must get home to score.

————

You cannot bring about prosperity by discouraging thrift.

You cannot strengthen the weak by weakening the strong.

You cannot help small men by tearing down big men.

You cannot help the poor by destroying the rich.

You cannot lift the wage-earner by pulling down the wage-payer.

You cannot keep out of trouble by spending more than your income.

You cannot further the brotherhood of man by inciting class hatred.

You cannot establish sound security on borrowed money.

You cannot build character and courage by taking away man's initiative.

You cannot really help men by having government tax them to do for them what they can and should do for themselves.

—Abraham Lincoln

———

"Say, you're fishing with last year's license," the fish and game warden startled a man.

"That's all right," came the dejected reply. "I'm only trying to catch the big one that got away last year."

How many of us are still trying to do this season's task equipped with only last year's programs and tools?

ACTIVITY

Two fathers, living on the same street, were each blessed with a goodly number of sons.

When one man wanted a job of work done he would say, "Go, boys, and do that."

But his neighbor, seeing the problem in his own home, would say, "Come, boys, let us do this together."

Knute Rockne, the famous football coach, once met one of his fourth-string players on the street, and said: "Quick now, it's the last play of the game. We're on the one yard line and behind by a score of six to nothing. What would you do?"

"Why, Coach," the man said without hesitation, "I'd move down to the far end of the bench to get a better view. I'd sure like to see that play."

The question is—are we content to sit on the bench and watch the play, while we should be in there carrying the ball ourselves?

————

Three words were written on the bulletin board of the chapel foyer:

Activity Is Contagious

————

AGE

Youth is not a time of life; it is a state of mind. It is not a matter of rosy cheeks, red lips; it is a temper of the will, a quality of imagination, a vigor of the emotions.

People grow old by deserting their ideals. Years wrinkle the skin, but to give up enthusiasm wrinkles the soul. Worry, doubt, self-distrust, fear and despair—these are the long, long years that bow the heart and turn the spirit back to dust. Whether sixty or sixteen, there is in every human being's heart the love of wonder, the undaunted challenge of events, the unfailing childlike appetite for what comes next and the joy of the game of living. We are as young as our faith, as old as our hope, as young as our self-confidence, as old as our fear; as young as our hopes, as old as our despair.

———————

Someone asked a woman how it was she kept her youth so wonderfully. Her hair was snowy white, she was eighty years old, and her energy was waning; but she never impressed one with the idea of her age, for her heart was still young in sympathy and interests. This was her answer:

"I know how to forget disagreeable things. I have tried to master the art of saying pleasant things. I do not expect too much of my friends. I have kept my nerves well in hand. I do not allow my thoughts to bore other people. I have always tried to find any work that came to hand congenial. I have retained the ideals of my youth, and did not later believe every man to be a liar and every woman spiteful. I have done my best to relieve the misery I came in contact with, and sympathized with suffering. In fact, I have tried to do to others as I would be done by, and you see me in consequence reaping the fruits of happiness and a peaceful old age."

———————

ATTITUDE

Man and boy he had worked for the town's leading mercantile institution for seventy years. He had enjoyed every day of it, but the highlight for him each year seemed to be participation in the employees' annual Christmas cantata.

Now he was growing old, and he knew that this Christmas might be his last year on the job. He began early, enthusiastically speaking to his fellow employees about their participation in the cantata. And hardly anyone could remember when a greater number of employees had faithfully attended the practices for the presentation.

During the dress rehearsal the store's manager, who had volunteered as the group's musical director, put down his baton and the music stopped.

"Mr. Brown," he turned to the old gentleman, "all during these rehearsals I've seen your mouth move, but I don't believe that I've heard you sing a note."

"Well, you see, sir," the man straightened up to the majesty of his full height, "my singing voice has been gone for years, but with a worthy project of this kind, I wanted to give it every ounce of support that I had."

————

Truly it has been written: "A little oil will do more to start the most stubborn machinery than all the vinegar in the world."

————

BEAUTY

A little girl skipping along at her father's side on an evening walk kept looking intently at the stars. Though apparently fascinated, she made no comment. Finally her father asked about what she was thinking.

"If the bottom side of heaven is so beautiful," she replied, "how wonderful the top side must be."

————

Nothing of beauty dies without having purified something, nor can aught of beauty be lost. Let us not be afraid of sowing it along the road. It may remain there for weeks or years but, like the diamond, it cannot dissolve, and finally there will

pass someone whom its glitter will attract. He will
pick it up and go his way rejoicing. Then why keep
back a lofty, beautiful word, for that you doubt
others will understand? An instant of higher
goodness was impending over you. Why hinder its
coming, even though you believe not that those
about you will profit thereby? What if you are
among the men of the valley? Is that sufficient
reason for checking the instinctive movement of
your soul toward the mountain peaks?

—Maurice Maeterlinck

————

Have you felt the pain of beautiful things?
    'Tis a pain that oftentimes comes to me,
Just as though some hand on the very heartstrings
    Were playing an air in a minor key.

Have you felt the pain of beautiful things,
    When the long wheat bends to the western
        breeze;
When the sunlight falls on butterfly wings,
    When the gold of autumn touches the trees?

Whence comes this pain of beautiful things?
    It comes at the bidding of God above;
As seed in the soil, in the heart it springs,
    And grows to a yearning for His love.

—Anonymous

————

BIBLE

Billy Sunday (1862-1935), the major-league baseball player turned evangelist, encouraged listeners to read the Bible and dig into it for spiritual truths. He often used the illustration of the diamond mines in South Africa and said that people all over the world knew about those mines, but only those who would go there to dig for them got the diamonds.

———

I was talking with a man one day, and he said he could not accept the statements in the scriptures about the fall of Adam, and death being brought into the world. He could not believe in the miracles recorded in the scriptures.

He said to believe that Joshua commanded the sun and the moon to stand still and that Jonah was swallowed by a fish was unscientific. "You cannot expect me to believe such things as these."

He thought himself consistent with reason, and that I was inconsistent. All of you go back with me, in imagination, to the year 1830, when the Church was organized.

Suppose I tell you—in 1830—that in the num-

ber of years between 1830 and today—that the
scientific marvels that we now know would be
commonplace. Will you accept that more quickly
than the story of Joshua or of Jonah? In 1830,
which story would you accept first?

—President Joseph Fielding Smith

———

It is one thing to read the Bible through,
Another thing to read and learn and do.
Some read it with design to learn to read,
But to the subject pay but little heed.

Some read it as their duty once a week,
But no instructions from the Bible seek;
While others read it with but little care,
With no regard to how they read nor where.

Some read to bring themselves into repute,
By showing others how they can dispute;
While others read because their neighbors do;
To see how long 'twill take to read it through.

Some read it for the wonders that are there—
How David killed a lion and a bear;
While others read it with uncommon care,
Hoping to find some contradiction there.

Some read as if it did not speak to them,
But to the people of Jerusalem.
One reads with father's specs upon his head,
And sees the things just as his father said.

Some read to prove a preadopted creed,
Hence understand but little that they read;
For every passage in the book they bend
To make it suit that all-important end.

Some people read, as I have often thought,
To teach the book instead of being taught;
And some there are who read it out of spite.
I fear there are but few who read it right.

—Anonymous

BLESSINGS

There is no doubt that every difficult thing that God permits to come into our lives has a blessing wrapped up in it. The things which appear before us as discouragements prove to be helps toward nobler attainments.

A physician, whose career had been full of faith and noble ministrations, gave this experience: He was a poor boy, and a cripple. One day he was watching some other boys on the ballfield. They were active, strong, and healthy. As he looked on, his heart grew bitter with envy.

A young man who stood beside him noted the discontent on his face, and said to him, "You wish you were in those boys' place, don't you?"

"Yes, I do," was the answer.

"I reckon God gave them money, education, and health," continued the young man, "to help them to be of some account in the world. Did it ever strike you," he paused a moment, "that He gave you a lame leg for the same reason—to make a man of you?"

The boy gave no answer, and turned away. He was angry, but he did not forget the words. His crippled leg God's gift! To teach him patience, courage, perseverance! To make a man of him! He thought of the words till he saw their meaning.

That kindled hope and cheer, and he determined to conquer his hindrance. He grew heroic. He soon learned that what was true of his lame leg was true also of all the difficulties, hindrances, and difficult conditions of life—they were all God's gifts to him to help him to be of some account in the world, to make a man of him.

———

BOOK OF MORMON

Some of you have heard President Nicholas G. Smith [later an Assistant to the Council of the Twelve], when he was president of the California Mission, tell us about how he was invited by the Dean of Religion at the University of Southern California in Los Angeles to let him take a copy of the Book of Mormon, and he gave him one that had been marked by the elders.

Then the Dean invited Brother Smith and the missionaries to come and listen to his sermon. He held up that Book of Mormon; he read verse after verse that had been marked by the elders, and he said this:

"I have here a volume of scripture which has been in our midst for a hundred years, and we have not known about it."

He read many passages which the elders had marked, and said: "This is not a dead book; it lives. Isn't it beautiful? Why can we not fellowship a people who believe in the beautiful things I have read to you today?"

—Elder LeGrand Richards

In the early 1830's the Nez Perce and Flathead Indians of Oregon sent four of their chiefs from Oregon to St. Louis, Missouri, to find a book. The story of their quest, as told by Archer Butler Hulbert in *Pilots of the Republic,* also by William A. Mowry in *Marcus Whitman,* runs thus:

Having learned that the white man had a book which came from heaven and which told him how to live, and of the future life, etc., these Indians held a great meeting, probably in the spring of 1832, and chose two old and two young men to go back and visit their "Father," General William Clark, at St. Louis, and get the Book. How or where they got this information no one knows, but the news of it seemed to impress them as something certain and of great meaning.

When they reached there it seems they could not find that book. The Bible was not the one they sought. These four Indians remained in and around St. Louis during the winter, and returned in the spring. General Clark told General Catlin that the only object of the coming of those Indians was to get the "Book from Heaven," and some say, to "meet men near to God."

Two of the chieftains died that winter. The other two, failing in their quest, returned soul-sick because of their failure. General Clark, who was the Clark of the Lewis and Clark Expedition, banqueted these two chiefs just before their return. At the dinner one of the chiefs arose and addressed General Clark. General Clark said that the address was taken verbatim by one of his interpreters. These were his pathetic words:

"I came to you over a trail of many moons from the setting sun. You were the friend of my fathers, who have all gone the long way. I came with one eye partly opened, for more light for my people, who sit in darkness. I go back with both eyes closed. How can I go back blind to my people? I made my way to you with strong arms, through many enemies and strange lands, that I might carry back much to them. I go back with both arms broken and empty.

"The two fathers who came with me—the braves of many winters and wars—we leave asleep here by your great water. They were tried in many moons and their moccasins wore out.

"My people sent me to get the white men's Book from Heaven. You took me where you allow your women to dance, as we do not ours, and the Book was not there. You took me where they worship the Great Spirit with candles, and the Book was not there. You showed me the images of good spirits and pictures of the good land beyond, but the Book was not among them.

"I am going back the long, sad trail to my people of the dark land. You make my feet heavy with burdens of gifts, and my moccasins will grow old in carrying them, but the Book is not among them. When I tell my poor blind people, after one more snow, in the big council that I did not bring the Book, no word will be spoken by our old men or by our young braves. One by one they will rise up and go out in silence.

"My people will die in darkness, and they will go on the long path to the other hunting grounds. No white man will go with them and no white man's book, to make the way plain. I have no more words."

———

BROTHERHOOD

President Heber C. Kimball once told the pioneers:

"The large roots of a tree receive their nourishment through the little fibers, and they receive it from the fountain; and then that nourishment is sent through the main trunk of the tree into the limbs, branches, and twigs. It is just so with the Church of Christ."

And President Brigham Young amplified:

"Brother Kimball most beautifully compared this people to a tree, remarking that we all receive nourishment from the same fountain. A tree shoots forth; it soon begins to have branches; but you cannot find two limbs precisely alike. A branch puts forth to bear fruit; the tree continues its course upwards; another branch starts out; and if it is a little different from the first branch, should it find fault and complain of the tree because of that difference in shape and capacity? You cannot find two twigs alike. You may examine any tree of the forest and see whether you can find any two leaves that are precisely alike. You cannot. Then you may go to a meadow, and see whether you can find two spears of grass just alike in shape and form. There are no two precisely alike. Examples of that endless variety are now before me.

"The greatest lesson you can learn is to learn yourselves. When we learn ourselves, we learn our neighbors. When we know precisely how to deal with ourselves, we know how to deal with our neighbors."

———

One day, as Count Tolstoy, the famed Russian

writer of another age, went out of the palace he
saw a beggar at the gates. The man looked so
miserable that Tolstoy felt in his pocket for a coin.
He fumbled in every pocket, but failed to find
one.

Sadly he said, "I have nothing for you today,
brother," and went on his way.

An hour later he returned and found the beggar
standing in the old place. He looked no longer
miserable, but warm, glowing and happy.

"What made this change?" asked Tolstoy.

The man replied, "Thanks to you."

"But I gave you nothing."

"No," said the beggar, "but you called me
friend and brother."

———

Have you looked for sheep in the desert,
    For those who have missed their way?
Have you been in the wild waste places,
    Where the lost and the wandering stray?
Have you trodden the lonely highway,
    The foul and the darksome street?

It may be you'd see in the gloaming
    The print of my wounded feet.

Have you folded home to your bosom
    The trembling, neglected lamb,
And taught to the little lost one
    The sound of the Shepherd's name?
Have you searched for the poor and the needy,
    With no clothing, no home, no bread?
The Son of Man was among them—
    He had nowhere to lay His head.

Have you carried the living water
    To the parched and thirsty soul?
Have you said to the sick and the wounded,
    "Christ Jesus make thee whole!"
Have you told my fainting children
    Of the strength of my Father's hand?
Have you guided the tottering footsteps
    To the shore of the golden land?

Have you stood by the sad and the weary,
    To smooth the pillow of death,
To comfort the sorrow-stricken
    And strengthen the feeble faith?
And have you felt, when the glory
    Has streamed through the open door,
And flitted across the shadow,
    That there I had been before?

Have you wept with the broken-hearted
    In their agony of woe?
Ye might hear Me whisper beside you
    "It's the pathway I often go!"
My brethren, My friends, My disciples,
    Can you always follow Me?
Then, wherever the Master dwelleth,
    There shall the servant be!

—Anonymous

———

CHARACTER

"You know," an old gentleman said, "when I had my picture taken recently I discovered a great truth: that photographer took a great deal more time looking for my best side than he did in taking my picture after he was certain he had found it. And I guess there have been acquaintances for whose best side I should have taken more time to look before I formed some hasty but lasting mental pictures of their abilities."

———

If you can't be a pine on the top of the hill,
    Be a scrub in the valley—but be

The best little scrub by the side of the rill;
    Be a bush if you can't be a tree.

If you can't be a bush, be a bit of the grass,
    And some highway much happier make;
If you can't be a muskie, then just be a bass—
    But the liveliest bass in the lake!

We can't all be captains, there has to be crew;
    There's something for all of us here;
There's big work to do and there's lesser to do,
    And the task we must do is the near.

If you can't be a highway, then just be a trail;
    If you can't be the sun, be a star;
It isn't by size that you win or you fail—
    Be the best of whatever you are!

—Douglas Malloch

I am not sure that we all understand our own characters. Indeed I am rather inclined to think that some of us are not on as good visiting terms with ourselves as we ought to be. I think it would be well for us to talk with ourselves sometimes and take stock of our condition.

You may call to mind Doctor Holmes' story of

his friend John. He said: "I like my friend John. He is an interesting fellow. By the way, there are three of him. In the first place there is the John that John knows. In the second place there is the John that John's friends know; and he is a very different John from the other one. And in the third place there is the John that only John's God knows."

So you see that when we are alone we need not be in solitude; there are two others of us to talk with; and if that conversation and self-communion be conducive to character building, to the uplifting of the soul, it were well that we be alone oftener than we are.

—Elder James E. Talmage

———

A man was once described as follows: "He's just a human dynamo that someone forgot to turn on!"

———

A ten-year-old son accompanied his father to get some seed grain from a neighbor. The neighbor was not home. When the neighbor was found, he responded: "Why did you not go and get it? I trust you. I would just as soon you would get it without me as with me. You go now and get the wheat seed. I'm busy. I cannot go right now, and you need the seed today."

As the man and his son were sacking the grain, the boy said: "Daddy, I would like, when I am a man, that men will say of me the same as our neighbor said of you today."

———

CHARITY

The total picture of true charity was given in a phrase by President George Albert Smith as he addressed the saints at the October 1949 general conference. He said simply: "They who give to the poor, but lend to the Lord."

———

An old lady sat in her old arm-chair
With wrinkled visage and disheveled hair
    And hunger-worn features:
For days and for weeks her only fare,
As she sat there in her old arm-chair,
    Had been potatoes.

But now they were gone; of bad or good
Not one was left for the old lady's food
    Of those potatoes.
And she sighed and said, "What shall I do?
Where shall I send, and to whom shall I go
    For more potatoes?"

And she thought of the deacon over the way,
The deacon so ready to worship and pray,
    Whose cellar was full of potatoes;
And she said, "I will send for the deacon to come;
He'll not mind much to give me some
    Of such a store of potatoes."

And the deacon came over as fast as he could,
Thinking to do the old lady some good,
    But never for once of potatoes:
He asked her at once what was her chief want,
And she, simple soul, expecting a grant,
    Immediately answered, "Potatoes."

But the deacon's religion didn't lie that way:
He was more accustomed to preach and to pray,
    Than to give of his hoarded potatoes:
So not hearing, of course, what the old lady said,
He rose to pray, with uncovered head,
    But she only thought of potatoes.

He prayed for patience, and wisdom, and grace,
But when he prayed "Lord give her peace,"
   She audibly sighed "Give potatoes;"
And at the end of each prayer which he said,
He heard, or thought that he heard in its stead,
   The same request for potatoes.

The deacon was troubled; knew not what to do;
'Twas very embarrassing to have her act so
   About "those carnal potatoes."
So ending his prayer, he started for home;
But, as the door closed behind him he heard a
     deep groan,
   "O, give to the hungry, potatoes!"

And that groan followed him all the way home;
In the midst of the night it haunted his room—
   "O, give to the hungry, potatoes!"
He could bear it no longer; arose and dressed,
From his well-filled cellar taking in haste
   A bag of his best potatoes.

Again he went to the widow's lone hut:
Her sleepless eyes she had not yet shut;
But there she sat in that old arm-chair,
With the same wan features, the same sad air.
And entering in, he poured on the floor
A bushel or more from his goodly store
   Of choicest potatoes.

The widow's heart leaped up for joy;
Her face was haggard and wan no more.
"Now," said the deacon, "shall we pray?"
"Yes," said the widow, "*now* you may."
And he kneeled him down on the sanded floor,
Where he had poured his goodly store,
And such a prayer the deacon prayed
As never before his lips essayed;
No longer embarrassed, but free and full,
He poured out the voice of a liberal soul,
And the widow responded aloud "Amen!"
But said no more of potatoes.

And would you, who hear this simple tale,
Pray for the poor, and praying "prevail,"
Then preface your prayers with alms and good
deeds:
Search out the poor, their wants and their needs;
Pray for peace, and grace, and spiritual food,
For wisdom and guidance, for all these are good,
But don't forget the potatoes.

—Rev. J. T. Pettee

————

A gentleman was one day relating to a Quaker a circumstance of deep distress that he had come across, and concluded very pathetically by saying: "I could not but feel for him."

"Verily, friend," replied the Quaker, "thou didst right in that thou didst feel for thy neighbor, but didst thou feel in the right place—didst thou feel in thy pocket?"

CHASTITY

I remember as a teen riding up South Fork of Ogden River on a dusty road near my home in Huntsville, Utah. Then there were no paved roads. Spring Creek was gurgling off by one side. Wild rose bushes were adorning the highway, but their blossoms were covered by the dust of every traveler and by the men with their heavy wagons who hauled the lumber down that old street.

I did not stop to pluck a rose along the highway, but a mile up I turned to the left into the meadow, just below a mountain canal. There was the same kind of roses blooming in the light of sunshine and kissed only by the morning dew, unsullied by the dust of every traveler passing by.

That was the rose I got off my horse to pluck, and I thought, "That is the kind of girl I should like to choose some day for my wife—one aside, pure, and spotless, untouched by the flying dust that had passed by."

That is the kind of girl every young man would like to choose if he has the love of truth in his heart; if he has within him the love of honor and beauty and pure virtue.

—President David O. McKay

————

CHILDREN

It was the kind of a home where the children were sent to church while Daddy stayed around the house, enjoying his paper in his well-worn slippers. And because Daddy hated to be alone, Mother always stayed with him.

But one morning as one of the children was being hurried out of the door the young man asked the question: "Mom, did Daddy go to Sunday School when he was like me?"

"Why, of course he did," replied Mother. "Why do you ask?"

"Because I don't think going to Sunday School will do me any good, either."

————

"Who winned?" a small child asked a returning, slightly-larger brother.

The mother didn't have to ask questions—she saw the dejected look on her son's face. And then it brightened as he answered the question:

"It wasn't really a winned—it was more like a hurricane!"

———

Yes, I know there are stains on my carpet,
  The traces of small muddy boots;
And I see your fair tapestry glowing,
  All spotless with flowers and fruits.

And I know that my walls are disfigured
  With prints of small fingers and hands!
And that your own household most truly
  In immaculate purity stands.

And I know that my parlor is littered
  With many odd treasures and toys,
While your own is in daintiest order,
  Unharmed by the presence of boys.

And I know that my room is invaded
  Quite boldly all hours of the day;

While you sit in yours unmolested
  And dream the soft quiet away.

Yes, I know there are four little bedsides
  Where I must stand watchful each night,
While you may go out in your carriage
  And flash in your dresses so bright.

Now, I think I'm a neat little woman;
  And I like my house orderly, too;
And I'm fond of all dainty belongings,
  Yet I would not change places with you.

No! keep your fair home with its order,
  Its freedom from bother and noise;
And keep your own fanciful leisure,
  But give me my four splendid boys.

—Anonymous

—————

CHRISTMAS

Christmas is a glad and welcome time because it is a season of kindly ministries. Much of the joy of Christmas-tide is a reflected joy, a joy flung back to us from the hearts which we have gladdened by some kindly deed. At that season we realize the sweetness and the benison of the God-appointed law that we cannot bless others without ourselves being blessed. It is ordained that no deed of mercy can go forth from human creatures without enriching the spirit of the worker, and that "he that watereth others shall himself be watered." And truly, if Christmas means anything at all it means love. Christ came to our world to pour divine kindness on weary, needy human lives. And the Christmas spirit, if it be truly present in our hearts, will send us out on the same mission. There is need everywhere for love's sweet ministry.

Let us light the lamp of heavenly charity and carry it through the wintry streets. Let us remember that in these chilly days the smallest act which brings comfort has a higher virtue than when summer laughs under the clear blue sky.

———

We return [at the Christmas season] to marvel at His achievement. There is nothing else like it in the annals of history:

Born in a manger.

Reared in Nazareth, concerning which place the

question was raised, "Can there any good thing come out of Nazareth?"

Reputed son of a carpenter.

Confined His personal ministry to Palestine.

Lived only thirty-three years.

Spent only three years in active ministry.

Headed no army—no political organization.

Amassed no wealth.

Literally "Had no place to lay His head."

Heralded no discovery.

Preached simply.

Assisted by lowly apostles.

Left no written record.

Scorned and despised of men.

Forgotten by one of His nearest, Peter.

Betrayed by His own, Judas.

Condemned to death along with criminals.

All this—and yet what glory He has achieved!

—Elder Adam S. Bennion

CHURCH

There was once a man who lived in a sleepy little village near a city. The city grew and became a metropolis, and the sub-dividers came to the village and it was neither sleepy nor village any more.

Commenting upon the turn of events the man said: "You know, those sub-dividers have put in so many new roads and streets that I feel that I must go home every night if I don't want to get lost getting home. I was recently away on a business trip for a month, and when I returned I felt lost as I drove to my home, passing residences on streets that I never knew existed. All good new homes filled with good people, mind you."

And some of us may feel the same way about the wonderful new programs being introduced by the Church. They are good, they are needed, but if we have missed going to several of the Church meetings, we feel lost and have to become re-acquainted.

———

I am reminded of an old legend. It runs in this wise:

At the time the persecutions were raging so bitterly against the early Saints, seven youths sought escape in a remote and lonely cave. After a time the Lord mercifully permitted them to fall asleep; and so deep and long was their slumber that they did not waken until two hundred years had passed.

When they were aroused from their sleep they went forth into the city of Ephesus, to which they belonged, and timidly they began to ask of the people if there were any Christians in the city.

"Christians!" was the response, "why, we are all Christians," and as evidence of it they pointed out the beautiful churches surmounted by the cross, wherein the worship of God was held; and as these young men visited the schools of learning they found the principles of the gospel there taught according to the written word.

They found it popular to be Christians, instead of unpopular, as it was when they hid themselves. Emperors with their wealth, professors with their learning, even the humble workmen, were followers of the cross and professed disciples of Jesus.

For a time they greatly rejoiced in the changed condition of things; but as they mingled among the people they found that while the professions were abundant, the spirit of the gospel was not with them, the signs and gifts of faith were not manifested among the people, and sorrowfully they retired to their cave, where their prayers moved God to take them unto Himself.

—Elder Abraham H. Cannon

CHURCH WELFARE

In the early days of the Church welfare program, Elmer G. Petersen, who was then president of the Utah State Agricultural College at Logan, was on our agricultural committee with Brother John A. Widtsoe as the chairman. We had sent him out on some kind of an agricultural assignment, and when he came back he prefaced his report by a rather significant statement. "Well,

I have discovered again something that I have already known. The members of this Church are like soldiers in the ranks, and all they need is for someone to give them marching orders."

—President Harold B. Lee

————

We should never fail, when we have it in our power and the opportunity presents itself, to administer to the wants of the poor and the needy; or, what is still better, devise ways and means which will enable them to administer to their own necessities. The latter is always preferable. Those who are the Lord's poor always prefer to provide for their own necessities than to be dependent upon others. They who are able to provide for themselves, but would rather have others bear the burdens of life for them, are not the Lord's poor, they are the devil's poor. They covet their neighbor's property—his food, house, horse and carriage. . . . They desire that which he possesses, without going to and earning them as he has done. It is not he who is most successful in gathering around him the goods of this life, who is always the most covetous.

—Elder Erastus Snow

————

CONDUCT

"Guilt by association" has been a long-standing problem.

Elder George A. Smith of the Council of the Twelve, later of the First Presidency, addressed the fifth anniversary of the coming of the pioneers to Utah, recalling ". . .the good old Quaker when he turned the dog out of doors: said he, 'I won't kill thee, thou hast got out of my reach; I cannot kill thee, but I will give thee a bad name;' and he hallooed out 'bad dog,' and somebody, supposing the dog to be mad, shot him."

———

In admonishing the Saints to strive to do better in pioneer Utah, President Jedediah M. Grant recalled an old circuit-riding Protestant "preacher" in Virginia. He came and preached in a certain place; the next time he came round a drunken man came staggering up to him and said, 'Brother Jones, when you was in our settlement you converted my soul.' 'Well,' said Brother Jones, 'I should think I did, for I do not believe the Lord had anything to do with it.' "

———

CRITICISM

From a pioneer general conference sermon of President Heber C. Kimball:

"I know it is very common for us to make observations like this when any of the brethren are chastised: Well, I guess some of the brethren have received a pretty good chastisement today, but it don't touch me. Don't you know that this is very common. That jacket does not suit me, says one. Why did it not suit you? Because you did not put it on. If you had put it on, it would have been like a piece of raw hide or a piece of India-rubber, then it would have pinched when it became dry. Now I do not believe that there is a person here who might not be benefited by these lessons of correction and instructions, for we can all make improvement in ourselves. . . ."

———

When we hear criticism leveled at a newly-announced goal, we are reminded of this old story:

A fine ship, well manned and officered, was leaving port, towing behind a small boat with a single occupant, who was thus enjoying a sail.

The man in the small boat looked ahead, and discovered signs of an approaching storm, and shouted: "Captain!"

The Captain of the large vessel shouted: "What is it?"

"Put back," said the single occupant of the small boat.

"What for?" asked the Captain.

"Storm coming, don't you see?"

"Yes, I see," called the Captain, "but I'm going where I'll have sea room."

"Put back, I tell you," persisted the man behind.

"Don't bother me with any more of that nonsense," the Captain shouted.

"Look here, Captain," came the determined reply; "if you don't put back, blowed if I don't cut you loose and let you go overboard."

And with a knife the man severed the tow rope, and the small boat drifted behind, while the ship sailed steadily on.

———

DEATH

He loved light, liberty, and little children.

A mighty leader he was, that loved to be led.

He was a master whose greatest joy was to serve.

Forgetful often he was of himself, but of his duties or his friends, never.

A peacemaker was he, and as a child of God, his first good morning and his last good night were to the Lord.

He was a warrior who never planned for a retreat.

He secured a title to an inheritance of earth under the provisions of the "Sermon on the Mount."

He had no time to make money, every moment was used in making manhood.

He died immensely rich, simply by keeping his account with the Lord straight.

His public speaking was the going out of one soul to the uplifting and warming of another.

His teaching was the leading of others to more knowledge, higher tastes, and nobler conduct.

His correction was a kindness that set conscience to cutting out evil.

In his nature the lion and the lamb lived together.

He was not famous for his flashes of success, but for his constancy. He struggled *to be* rather than *to seem.* He placed much more value on preparation than on position.

He was a fixed star, and those who took their bearings from it and held to the course of safety indicated by the reckonings made therefrom, have never been shipwrecked, nor has a single one of them missed entrance at the golden gate of success.

His faith had three chief objects on which it rested: his God, his fellowman, and himself.

He sought earnestly two things: the will of the Lord and how best to do that will.

—Elder George H. Brimhall,
on the passing of Elder Karl G. Maeser

———

There are men here who know him better, but none who had a warmer heart for him than I. I love his memory—it will always be an incentive and an inspiration to me.

—Elder Orson F. Whitney,
of President Francis M. Lyman

FAITH

Faith is like a flame in the heart of man, it gives us confidence in God's divine purpose, his everlasting watchfulness, his promise for the eternities.

Upon the firm foundation of faith man aspires to the heights in every facet of achievement.

Through faith, endeavor gains true purpose; accomplishment becomes the serene fulfillment in an understanding of man's mission and his partnership with God.

Through a world-wide missionary system, through temples and chapels, schools, academies, seminaries, and university; through the medium of mass information, but mostly in the lives of its members, The Church of Jesus Christ of Latter-day Saints carries the testimony of love, culture, peace, brotherhood, wisdom and compassion to all peoples as fruits of the gospel of Christ.

Our faith sustains the conviction that indeed God does live, that Jesus is his begotten Son, divine and eternal.

It fervently teaches that through the gospel of Christ all men may be saved through obedience to its principles, and that only through an honest and sincere application of its teachings can a lasting peace ever come to a troubled world.

———

Faith is the key to knowledge rare,
God's choice and priceless gift to man;
It is obtained in humble prayer
And practice of the gospel plan.

It opens the door to secrets deep—
Communes with God, in nature's sleep.
Prevails with God, till mortal man
The glory of the Lord can scan.

—From "The Gospel Pioneer,"
by Elder William Jefferies

———

In pioneering Utah, President Brigham Young recalled a "young man in Nauvoo who sat down to breakfast from a Johnny cake [corn bread] alone; [and] says he, 'I do not ask a blessing on this; if God does not give me better food than this, I shall never ask him to bless it.' "

President Young recalled his answer to the young man as being: "You will make a shipwreck of your faith!"

———

All that I have seen teaches me to trust the Creator for all that I have not seen.

—Ralph Waldo Emerson

———

FAMILY

A little bird sat on a cherry-tree limb,
And a dear little maiden listened to him;
For each word of his song, though loud and clear,
Was meant for nobody else's ear.
"Sweet! sweet!" he said, "You'll surely agree—
The man the head of the house should be."

"That's all very well for a bird, you know,"
The maiden answered in whispers low;
"But a woman, I think, has a right to reign
As a sovereign queen of her own domain!"
"Sweet! sweet!" sang the little bird saucily,
"The man the head of the house should be."

"But what if it happens," the maiden said,
"That the very one I may choose to wed,
Though worthy of love, is too weak to rule—
For even a man may be a fool!"
"Sweet! sweet!" said the bird, ere she made her
    plea,
"The man the head of the house should be."

Away flew the bird to its cozy nest;
Deep, deep went his song to the maiden's breast.
And she found it true as the bird had sung,
In the summertime when the maid was young;

"The man the head of the house should be!
But the wife—the heart of the house is she!"

—Anonymous

———

Oh, give me patience when wee hands
Tug at me with their small demands.

And give me gentle and smiling eyes.
Keep my lips from hasty replies.

And let not weariness, confusion, or noise
Obscure my vision of life's fleeting joys.

So when, in years to come, my house is still—
No bitter memories its room may fill.

—Anonymous

———

FORGIVENESS

A man was telling his troubles to his bishop, and had reached his conclusion:

"There, bishop. With such a neighbor am I not right in feeling the way I do?"

"Yes, feeling the way you do is only human; but to forgive such a neighbor would be divine."

———

"Forgiveness and forgetting are but the two sides of the same coin," said a Sunday School teacher, "in fact, forgetting the incident is so much a part of forgiving that these two great words are inseparable."

———

I will tell you a circumstance that took place with me upwards of forty years ago. I was living in Canada at the time, and was a traveling Elder. I presided over a number of the churches in that district of country. A difficulty existed in a branch of the Church, and steps were taken to have the matter brought before me for settlement.

I thought very seriously about it, and thought it a very insignificant affair. Because we ought to soar above such things, and walk a higher plane, for we are children of God and should be willing to suffer wrong rather than do wrong; to yield a good deal to our brethren for the sake of peace and quietness, and to secure and promote good feelings among the Saints.

At that time I did not have the experience I now have [he was speaking during the long apostolic interim between the passing of President Brigham Young in August 1877 and the sustaining of President Taylor as President of the Church in October 1880], and yet I do not know that I could do any better than I did then. Before going to the trial I bowed before the Lord, and sought wisdom from him to conduct the affair aright, for I had the welfare of the people at heart.

When we had assembled I opened the meeting with a prayer, and then called upon a number of those present to pray; they did so, and the Spirit of God rested upon us. I could perceive that a great feeling existed in the hearts of those who had come to present their grievances, and I told them to bring forward their case. But they said they had not anything to bring forward.

The feelings and spirit they had been in possession of had left them, the Spirit of God had obliterated these feelings out of their hearts, and they knew it was right for them to forgive one another.

—President John Taylor

FREE AGENCY

You remember in the great tragedy, Goethe's
Faust just after the prologue in heaven has been
given, the curtain rises and shows the old study
built in Gothic style. The shelves of the room are
full of books and chemical apparatus. Faust is
sitting at a table pondering the first chapter of the
Gospel of St. John. He arises and gives these
famous words:

"All that philosophers can teach, the craft of
lawyer and a leach, I have mastered, and waded
through philosophy's dreary deserts, too, and yet,
poor fool, for all I care, I am not wiser than
before."

Then you call to mind how Faust, becoming
totally discouraged, finally sells his soul to Satan
on condition that he have new life and a chance to
work on life's problems over again. Faust becomes
a young man; he falls in love with Marguerite; he
sins. Marguerite, at the end of part one, dies.
Faust, still under the power of Mephistopheles,
wanders about the earth and finally, after having
seen the ages of the past and dreamed over the
ages of Homer and Virgil, wanders back to his old
study, but Mephistopheles is still behind him
holding him absolutely in control. But Faust is
awakened to a sense of his own power, after he

sees his old servant, Wagner, and turning to Mephistopheles, he says:

"Remember that from now on I am to redeem my soul from your power and control."

Mephistopheles asks him how he shall do it, and Faust replies: "There are two souls contending within me, one is trying to become master of the other, and I set out to have my redeeming soul become the master."

Here is the problem; here is the thought of Mormonism, ethically. There are two powers contending for the soul of man and man stands free to choose between them. After choosing right, the redemption of his own soul comes from his own hard toil, for as Faust points out, his soul cannot be redeemed [except] through work with a faith sublime in the higher law of God. Ethically speaking, then, Mormonism says that every child is divine; endowed with divine powers to become the master of himself and the intelligent interpreter of God's laws. He becomes his own redeemer; he works out his own salvation, but this is according to law—the religious law—and obedience to these laws with the freedom of his own soul gives him liberty, for obedience to law is liberty.

—Elder Reed Smoot

God is standing in the shadow of eternity, it seems to me, deploring now the inevitable results of the follies, the transgressions, and the sins of his wayward children, but we cannot blame him for these any more than we can blame a father who might say to his son:

"There are two roads, my son, one leading to the right, one leading to the left. If you take the one to the right, it will lead you to success and happiness. If you take the one to the left, it will bring you misery and unhappiness, and perhaps death, but you choose which you will. You must choose, I will not force either upon you."

The young man starts out and, seeing the allurements and the attractiveness of the road to the left, and thinking it a short cut to his happiness, he concludes to take it. The father knows what will become of him. He knows that not far from that flowery path there is a mire-hole into which his boy will fall; he knows that after he struggles out of that mire-hole he will come to a slough into which he will flounder. He sees others who have chosen that path in that same slough, and he knows that in their struggle to get on dry land there will be fighting. He could see it long before the boy reached that condition, and he could, therefore, foretell it. The father loves the boy just the same, and would still continue to warn him and plead for him to return to the right path.

God, too, has shown the world, through his prophets in ages gone by, that many of his people, individuals as well as nations, would choose the path that leads to misery and death, and he foretold it, but the responsibility is upon those who would not heed God's message, not upon God. But in his infinite wisdom, he will overrule these transgressors for the good of all his sons and daughters. His love for them is always manifest.

—President David O. McKay

———

FRIENDSHIP

Around the corner I have a friend
In this great city which has no end;

Yet, days go by and weeks rush on,
And before I know it a year has gone.

And I never see my old friend's face;
For life is a swift and terrible race.

He knows I like him just as well
As in the days when I rang his bell

And he rang mine. We were younger then
And now we are busy, tired men—

Tired with playing the foolish game;
Tired with trying to make a name;

Tomorrow, I say, I will call on Jim,
Just to show I'm thinking of him.

But tomorrow comes and tomorrow goes;
And the distance between us grows and grows.

Around the corner! Yet miles away—
Here's a telegram, sir—"Jim died today!"

And that's what we get—and deserve in the end—
Around the corner, a vanished friend.

—Anonymous

———

I would be true, for there are those who trust me;
I would be pure, for there are those who care;
I would be strong, for there is much to suffer;
I would be brave, for there is much to dare.

I would be friend of all—the foe, the friendless;
I would be giving, and forget the gift;

I would be humble, for I know my weakness;
I would look up—and laugh—and love—and lift.

—Howard Arnold Walters

———

One only Friend we have
　　Accounted sure;
One only love is ours
　　That will endure.

All other friends are dear:
　　He knows how dear
Who gave them for our joy
　　And solace here.

All other loves are sweet:
　　He knows how sweet
Of whom sad souls that lack
　　For love entreat.

But friends however true
　　This life will test,
And they will fail us oft
　　Who know us best.

All loves however strong
　　In time may change;

Misfortune may divide,
New ties estrange.

Surest of all will come
Some sad offense;
Mistrust will chill, and doubt
Divide friends hence.

Oh, slow of heart to learn
What yet we own—
One only perfect Friend
Hath any known!

—Anonymous

FUTILITY

According to legend, a certain Englishwoman, Mrs. Partington, had a cottage near the seashore. She is supposed to have tried to sop up with her mop the waves driven into her home by a heavy gale in November 1824.

"Dame Partington and her mop" became a famous symbol of persons who try to block progress or fight the inevitable. Sidney Smith, speaking in the House of Lords in 1831, said of her: "She was excellent at slop or puddle, but should never have meddled with a tempest."

―――

The novelist George Eliot had a character in *Adam Bede* say:

"It's but little good you'll do a-watering last year's crop."

―――

He has spent all his life in letting down buckets into empty wells; and in frittering away his age in trying to draw them up again.

—Sydney Smith

―――

A centipede was happy, quite,
Until a frog, in fun, said,
"Pray, which leg comes after which?"
This put his mind in such a pitch,
He lay distracted in a ditch,
Considering how to run.

—Anonymous

―――

GENEALOGY

When I went on my first mission to Holland, there were three of us who went to that land—a brother from Idaho, one from Spanish Fork, Utah, and myself. We landed in Rotterdam. One of them was sent up to the north. He had a German name and when he was called to go to Holland his people were disappointed, feeling that he ought to go to Germany where he could look up the genealogy of his father's people.

When he arrived in the northern part of Holland, what we call Groningen, he was sent out into the little city of Veendam, and he and his companion went looking for a place to live—furnished rooms.

This young man said to his companion, "This looks like a nice place; let's go in here."

After they were there a few weeks, he found that a record of his father's people had been brought across the border out of Germany, and his father's family never knew that their people had ever been in Holland.

Think of the inspiration of God that led the President of the Church to send that boy to

Holland, and the inspiration that guided the president of the mission to send him up into the north, and the inspiration that guided the district president to send him to the little city of Veendam, about 60,000 population at that time, and the same inspiration that led him and his companion to the very house where he found that record.

Now, he died over there with the smallpox. I was present at his burial. The city was going to burn the book because it had been handled by the deceased.

The district president said, "If you do, it will cost you five hundred dollars."

They said no book was worth that much, but they fumigated it page by page and sent it to the family. They did the temple work.

—Elder LeGrand Richards

———

Men and women are more than mere bricks in the sight of the Lord. They are his sons and daughters. But, like bricks, they must be pure, clean, and true, to be of the most value.

Then something else must happen, continuing this theme of likening men and women to bricks. They must be gathered into family patterns and then they must be sealed together, as bricks are fashioned with mortar into a solid wall. They must be gathered first in genealogical efforts, and then sealed together into one great whole, with the family pattern, in the temple activity.

————

It has been sagely stated: "The person who prates about his or her family tree usually has no idea of how much it needs pruning."

————

GOALS

A group of stake executives had been called together to hear about a new program being implemented by the Church. The opening song by the all-men congregation left much to be desired.

After the prayer the speaker of the meeting began his remarks with: "Your singing reminds me of this new program of the Church. You're a little unsure of the words at present, but you do recognize the tune."

————

"We never climb a tree by plucking at the blossoms," said a leader of youth. "To climb a tree we must grasp the limbs and then work our way to the top of the tree."

————

"What is the real good?"
I asked in musing mood;

"Order," said the law court;
"Knowledge," said the school;
"Truth," said the wise man;
"Pleasure," said the fool;
"Love," said the maiden;
"Beauty," said the page;
"Freedom," said the patriot;
"Home," said the sage;
"Fame," said the soldier;
"Equity," the seer.

Spake my heart full sadly:
"The answer is not here."

Then within my bosom,
Softly this I heard:
"Each heart holds the secret;
'Kindness' is the word."

—Anonymous

————

GOSPEL

The gospel is better than any human code of conduct; primarily because it not only tells man what is right, but gives him the strength to do the right. The wise man can say to another, "You are doing wrong," but he cannot give the wrongdoer the will to turn from the wrong. The moralist can graphically picture to the sinner the tragic end of the downward course, but he cannot nerve the sinner with the strength to break the shackles of his bondage. The gospel is stronger and truer than the wisest words of the wisest men, because it has the power to make bad men good and good men better.

—Elder Nephi Jensen

————

In the days when railroads offered the only sure way of long-distance travel there was a saying that "All trains go to Chicago." Some religionists built upon that, saying that "As all railroads lead to Chicago so all churches lead to heaven."

A young missionary had occasion to disagree with that way of thinking as he stood at the pulpit. He cited scripture that there was really only one way to heaven—active membership in The Church of Jesus Christ of Latter-day Saints.

Then continuing his theme he said something like this: "The ticket one must have on this road is faith. It cannot be used effectively on any other. A ticket made out for heaven will not get you there, if you board a train for hell, even though the conductor accepts your ticket and allows you to ride."

Then very humbly he concluded: "I am a conductor on God's great railroad. It is the only one that leads through the deep and sometimes uninviting valley of repentance, into the narrow pass of baptism, to the high plateau of basic truth, and then a straight line with the horizon ever-beckoning with more truth."

———

One time when I was in St. Augustine, Florida, I saw a sundial on the outside front wall of a church. That dial told the time to those outside the church but was of no service to those inside the church.

I sometimes think that we preach the gospel for

the benefit of outsiders and forget that we should have the benefit of it.

—Elder Charles A. Callis

GOVERNMENT

I remember well the late senator, Philander C. Knox of Pennsylvania, a member of the committee on Privileges and Elections of the Senate, coming to me one morning and asking me if The Church of Jesus Christ of Latter-day Saints believed in our [American] form of government. I told the senator we believed that the Constitution of the United States was an inspired instrument from God; we believed that the men who drafted and put it into force were inspired and directed by the overruling hand of God.

He asked: "Have you any declarations to show your belief?"

I called his attention first to the twelfth article of our faith. I read it to him, but it hardly satisfied him—that short statement—and he asked if there were not some written, published statement of the Church, showing its attitude toward the government and the laws of our land.

"Senator Knox," I said, "I will see that by tomorrow morning you will get a copy of the Doctrine and Covenants, and I ask you to turn to section 134 and read the section, and you will find there a clear, concise, straight-forward statement of the position of the 'Mormon' Church, so-called, toward the government of the United States and the laws of our country."

It satisfied him.

—Elder Reed Smoot

————

Some years ago, in Nauvoo, a gentleman in my hearing, a member of the Legislature, asked Joseph Smith how it was that he was enabled to govern so many people, and to preserve such perfect order; remarking at the same time that it was impossible for them to do it anywhere else.

[The Prophet] remarked that it was very easy to do that.

"How?" responded the gentleman; "to us it is very difficult."

[The Prophet] replied, "I teach them correct principles, and they govern themselves."

The above I have seen fully exemplified in different nations. In Manchester, England, I attended a conference a short time ago, at which there were assembled two or three hundred elders, and officers of various kinds, and some thousands of people; and in all of their business transactions I did not hear one dissenting voice.

We have also other laws, which we as citizens of the United States recognize. In Nauvoo, we had a city charter, city council, municipal court, made our city regulations, laws, etc.; but this was more for protection than otherwise.

At the present time we have a Territory in the United States, acknowledged by the Congress and President of the United States. We have our own Governor, Secretary of State, Legislature, and other government officers. These to us are a protection and a shield. We never find any difficulty in keeping the laws of the land; but as we have others who are not in the Church, nor subject to its laws, we have the means within our reach [civil law] of preventing one citizen interfering with another's rights, as well as preserving ourselves from being imposed upon; for we do not enforce our Church laws upon those who are not members of the Church. Everything with us is voluntary.

All men are protected with us in their religious rights, no matter what nation or creed they belong to. We teach men good principles; if they receive them, well; if not, it is their own business. We never persecute a person for his religious faith.

–President John Taylor
Millennial Star November 15, 1851
quoting *Etoile du Deseret*

HOLY GHOST

Latter-day Saints are, and have been, highly favored; the channel of communication has been opened from heaven to earth in our day, and has inspired this people with the gift of the Holy Ghost, and by that gift they have proved the things of God.

When I read the productions of men I am apt to forget them; I go for instance to Elder Orson Hyde's grammar class, and I study, and read, and commit the rules of grammar to memory, but unless I keep my mind constantly upon that subject, it will fly away from me.

On the contrary, there are certain truths brought to my mind by the Spirit of the Lord, that I have never forgotten. Truths deposited by the Holy Ghost are treasured up in the mind, and do not leave it.

—Elder Jedediah M. Grant

————

HOME TEACHING

[William Farrington Cahoon was born at Harpersfield, Ashtabule County, Ohio, November 7, 1813. He joined the Church October 16, 1830, and first met the Prophet that winter at Kirtland. In 1892, when the *Juvenile Instructor* recorded this testimony (Volume 27, Page 492), it said that Elder Cahoon had been a member of the Church longer than anyone then living.]

I was called and ordained to act as a teacher to visit the families of the Saints. I got along very well till I found that I was obliged to pay a visit to the Prophet. Being young, only about seventeen years of age, I felt my weakness in visiting the Prophet and his family in the capacity of a teacher. I almost felt like shrinking from the duty. Finally I went to his door and knocked, and in a minute the Prophet came to the door. I stood there trembling and said to him: "Brother Joseph,

I have come to visit you in the capacity of a teacher, if it is convenient for you."

He said, "Brother William, come right in; I am glad to see you; sit down in that chair there, and I will go and call my family in."

They soon came in and took seats. He then said, "Brother William, I submit myself and my family into your hands," and then took his seat. "Now, Brother William," said he, "ask all the questions you feel like."

By this time my fears and trembling had ceased, and I said, "Brother Joseph, are you trying to live your religion?"

He answered, "Yes."

I then said, "Do you pray in your family?"

He said, "Yes."

"Do you teach your family the principles of the gospel?"

He replied: "Yes, I am trying to do it."

"Do you ask a blessing on your food?"

He answered, "Yes."

"Are you trying to live in peace and harmony with all your family?"

He said that he was.

I turned to Sister Emma, his wife, and said, "Sister Emma, are you trying to live your religion? Do you teach your children to obey their parents? Do you try to teach them to pray?"

To all these questions she answered, "Yes, I am trying to do so."

I then turned to Joseph and said, "I am now through with my questions as a teacher; and now if you have any instructions to give, I shall be happy to receive them."

He said, "God bless you, Brother William, and if you are humble and faithful, you shall have power to settle all difficulties that may come before you in the capacity of a teacher."

I then left my parting blessing upon him and his family, as a teacher, and took my departure.

—Elder William Farrington Cahoon

HONESTY

In discussing the broad field of honesty, and how some apparently believed it was the thing to do to use the roads developed by another into the places where timber could be obtained, President Brigham Young once recalled that "these characters do as the old Quaker did when he whipped the man; he took off his coat, and said, 'Religion do thou lie there, until I whip this man.' The boys, or many of them, who go into the canyons with wagons and teams do the same; they lay down their religion at the mouth of the canyon, saying, 'Thou lie there, until I go for my load of wood.' "

HUMILITY

A young woman embraced the gospel in the north of Ireland a number of years ago. For a long time she had been hungering and thirsting after righteousness. The Lord knew this, and in his mercy he sent an elder to her with glad tidings which filled her soul with unquenchable joy. She was an invalid; she had not been able to use her limbs for years, and in other ways was greatly deformed.

A natural compassion for her filled the bosoms

of the Saints. We felt that here was a case on which the Lord ought to surely manifest his power. We would fast and pray in her behalf, that when she was baptized she might be healed. Fast and prayer meetings were held, and the Lord was implored (commanded would be nearer the truth) to heal her. The majority of all present felt that she would be healed, but some doubted. An over-zealous elder assured the young woman that as soon as she came up out of the water, she would be made whole in every way.

The morning of her baptism came. A number of the young lady's friends were invited to witness the ceremony, but more properly speaking, the coming miracle. A carriage was hired, and the young woman was driven to the public baths. There the driver was dismissed, told that his services would no longer be required, as the young lady was going to walk home. The proprietor of the baths was invited to witness the miracle.

A miracle was performed that day, but it was far different than we expected. The young woman was baptized and confirmed, but she was not healed. Something almost bordering on consternation seized some of the elders as they saw their promises fall to the ground unfulfilled.

The young woman looked up, her face beaming with joy, and said: "Brethren, don't feel bad. I have not been healed as you promised me I would be, but I have a stronger testimony than the testimony of healing. The Lord has fulfilled his promise, and has given me the testimony of his Holy Spirit, which bears witness with my spirit that I have done his holy will."

A hack was sent for, and the young woman was taken to her home, while we returned to our homes sadder but wiser men. A few months later, the dear young sister fell asleep in full fellowship of the Church.

"Why was she not healed?" you ask. One of the reasons was that we had gone contrary to the counsels of the Master, who, in revelation given to the Prophet Joseph, commanded the elders not to boast of these things before the world. (See D&C 105:24.) Yet this is what we had done. How could we expect the blessing?

Let us confine ourselves as missionaries to the first principles of the gospel; let the elders go out as did the Apostle Paul, professing to know nothing but Jesus Christ and him crucified. He,

Christ, is our great examplar, and if we follow in his steps, we will never go astray.

—Elder William A. Morton
writing in 1903

————

Humble we must be, if to Heaven we go:
High is the roof there; but the gate is low.

—Robert Herrick

————

The fruits of humility are love and peace.

—Hebrew Proverb

————

LEADERSHIP

Elder Spencer W. Kimball of the Council of the Twelve once told a roomfull of bishoprics that what he was drawing on the board was a slough. Here were trapped some of the finest people in the Church—the members of the Senior Aaronic Priesthood and those inactive for many reasons. It was the responsibility of the Church members to drain that slough and reclaim those members by warming them up, creating a desire within them to repent, fellowshipping them, and then to build dikes around that slough—dikes called Primary, Sunday School, MIA, seminary, and other activity —so strong that no other member would ever be trapped there again.

————

Upon one occasion Theodore Roosevelt was decorating one of his soldiers for bravery in the Spanish-American War. He said, "This is the bravest man I have ever seen. He walked right behind me all the way up San Juan Hill."

Theodore Roosevelt, who later became President of the United States, knew the meaning of good leadership.

————

The Mormon Pioneers in the Salt Lake Valley used to point to a favorite peak in the southeast and liken the Church and its leadership to it. The peak was often the point of storms and weather disturbances. Sometimes, from the Valley, the peak was hidden from view. But they knew that

that peak was unmoved and undisturbed, and that soon it could be seen again in all its majesty.

———

I call to your attention five major and five minor qualities of a leader.

1. The leader must have faith in his work.

The leader, first of all must have full faith in the cause he represents. Faith in the Church, faith in his superiors, faith in his fellowmen, faith in himself, faith that the work with which he has been entrusted will be done. Unless a leader has such faith, his battle is lost.

2. The leader must love his work.

Faith alone is insufficient; it must be qualified with love. There is a definite relationship between faith and love; but there is also a subtle distinction. The man who has faith, and adds to that faith a love for the work, for the cause, for his superiors, for his fellow workers, finds ecstasy in the labor. Such a man has won the second great quality of leadership, for love begets love, as the electrified coil of wire induces a current in the nearby coil.

3. The leader must understand his work.

Faith and love must be fed, and the best way to feed them is to acquire full knowledge concerning the work at hand. While his love will beget love in those with whom he associates, so will his knowledge, as he acquires it, make his fellow workers stronger than they would be without such knowledge.

4. The leader must be industrious and persistent.

Neither faith, nor love, nor knowledge, comes permanently except from labor. Industry is an indispensable quality of leadership. The man who will not pay the price in hard work cannot achieve leadership. Every great leader knows how to work, is willing to work industriously and persistently, and never knows defeat.

5. The leader is prayerful.

Every true leader knows his limitations. No leader is so foolish as to believe that he knows everything. No leader believes that, unaided, he can accomplish any great work placed upon him. A great leader is prayerful.

From these five major qualities of a leader, let me draw five minor ones:

1a. The leader is an optimist.

The man who has faith of necessity becomes an optimist. The leader sees possibilities, never impossibilities. He sees light; he does not dwell on the shadows. He sees good in his fellowmen; he seldom sees that which is evil. He trusts, and does not allow himself to distrust.

2a. The leader is generous and self-effacing.

He gives more than he receives. You remember the code of the old Vikings. The Viking chief rode the seas, and when the victory had been won, divided all the booty among his men; but not a thing did he take for himself. He who thinks of himself in the limelight, who does not share the public honors with his fellow workers, is not a true leader. "What is there in it for me?" is never asked by true leaders.

3a. The leader is self-reliant.

This quality is drawn out of knowledge. Though he depends on God, the leader believes that since he has been called to the office, if he does his duty well he will be able to accomplish

the work assigned. He is not afraid. He stands
self-reliantly before his task and before his fellowmen.

4a. The leader plans his work ahead.

This quality is intimately associated with the
quality of work. This is ordinarily called organization. Every good leader organizes his work, and
disdains to go to his work unprepared. He dreams
of his work by night, and he thinks of it by day,
and he throws it into such an organized form that
he knows where he is going all the time.

5a. The leader is a good follower.

Drawn out of prayer, out of communion with
God and the Spirit of God, is the personal quality
of being a good follower. The truly great man is
quite as willing to follow, as he is to lead; just as
willing to be directed, as to direct. Somewhere, for
every man, there is superior authority.

—Elder John A. Widtsoe

———

Many years ago, while I was presiding in the
Southern States Mission, Brother Sidney Teebles
of Holden, Utah, entered the mission field. He had

been concerned about his call, and had discussed it with his friend President Joseph F. Smith, who later became the sixth President of the Church.

The missionary-to-be wished that it had only been a call to work in his life work, the care of herds of sheep, bands of horses, or herds of cattle and calves; if that were the call, then he felt very certain that he could have accomplished something in it; but to be called to preach the gospel was something for which he considered himself entirely unfitted.

President Smith answered him: "Brother Teebles, when you can learn to love men as dearly as you now love stock calves, you can succeed in preaching the gospel."

That is the secret of success in missionary work, and also in leadership—to love the purpose for which you are working, the objective at which you aim.

—President B. H. Roberts

————

LIFE

When you have found your life, give it away.

Give it freely. Give it in the song that rests the heart of the weary, and whispers peace to the turbulent soul. Give it in the thought set to the Muse's music, that thrills, inspires, uplifts, and ennobles. Give it in unanswerable logic in Truth's defense, and Right's vindication. Give it in that sympathy which grieves at the sight of need, and sorrows when others are sad. Give it in that love which knoweth no self, but goeth about continually doing good. Give it to God in that devotion which recognizes his laws as supreme.

The greatest life which has been lived was a gift, and was spent in giving. ... [Christ's] was the perfect life. For he found his life and gave it away.

—Elder Nephi Jensen

————

Nobody has a right to find life uninteresting or unrewarding who sees within the sphere of his own activity a wrong he can help to remedy or within himself an evil he can hope to overcome.

—Charles William Eliot
"The Happy Life"

————

Today is your day and mine, the only day we have, the day in which we play our part. What our part may signify in the great whole we may not understand, but we are here to play it, and now is the time. This we know, it is a part of action, not of whining.

—David Starr Jordan

———

It was my privilege years ago to visit the Royal Academy in London, as one of a small body of invited guests conducted by distinguished hosts.

I do not claim to be a connoisseur in painting, but I was particularly attracted to one small canvas. It was a landscape, and the artist-guide who was with me was a specialist in landscape painting.

Having already openly and freely confessed my ignorance of the technique of art, I felt myself free to ask questions; so I said to my guide: "Please tell me something about that painting; it is rather puzzling to me."

My companion smiled and asked why I was especially interested. I replied that the painting was somehow unsatisfying. He said he was glad that I had asked him about it, and continued: "First tell me what you see in it."

I replied that it seemed to me to be well drawn and that the perspective seemed good. He agreed that it was well drawn and that the perspective was well-nigh perfect. Indeed, he proceeded to explain, it was obvious that the artist had studied perspective carefully, so devotedly indeed that an expert could tell just what books on the subject he had read, and the authors by whom he was most influenced.

My guide then asked me what I thought of the color, and I replied that it appealed to me. He rejoined that every rule of coloring had been carefully followed, that he was able to name the principal masters whom the artist had followed in the matter of color.

As I hesitated, he prompted me by asking, "What do you think of the composition?"

"Well," I said, "it seems to me to be a well balanced painting;" and he agreed with me.

Then I asked, "Is it a good painting?" and my guide answered forcefully, "No, it is not good."

I inquired then what was the matter with it, perspective, color, composition, all being according to rule.

"That painting," my companion averred, "lacks just—that!"

The last word was accompanied by a sweeping gesture of the hand.

I understood him. He meant that the painting was machine-made, that the artist had worked according to rule, not law. In fact, the painting was an imitation. My friend commented in an undertone that canvas, pigments, and oils are not enough to make a painting.

Later, as I communed with myself over the incident, I soliloquized: "Pigments and oils are not enough for a good painting; there must be some of the artist's own blood mixed in to make the canvas a masterpiece."

We must learn to give of ourselves. Think of the Christ. He gave of himself. A spark of his nature, of his very spirit, was in every word that he spoke, whether of instruction, condemnation, warning, or encouragement; and that is one reason why he is the One of all those who have ever trodden the earth of whom most has been said and sung. Aye, as the Son of the Living God, the Savior and Redeemer of the world, he could not have done otherwise.

—Elder James E. Talmage

―――――

LOVE

Love is the key which unlocks the human heart. Love is to the boy or girl what sunshine is to the blossoming earth, what rain is to the parched soil. Love is the builder of character, the bridge which spans misunderstandings. It kindles the spark of hope and fills the air with happy song. Love mends broken lives, changes deep sorrow to joy and is truly the life of the soul.

As long as we love, we serve. May our love be evidenced by the service we give.

―――――

A very modest young man had been paying attentions to a young woman. She thought he was not making the advances that she might reasonably expect. However, he took her on a day-long outing to a mining center, and when they were passing through a tunnel on the excursion car his arm fell about her waist. Then they suddenly emerged into broad daylight and his arm was still there for a fleeting moment.

The young man was greatly embarrassed, and rubbing his hands nervously, said: "Mary, do you know that this tunnel cost ten million dollars?"

"Did it?" she replied. "Well, it is worth it."

————

MAN

The great need of the present day and age is men; men who are not for sale; men who are honest, sound from center to circumference; true to the heart's core; men who will condemn wrong in friend or foe, and in themselves as well as others; men whose consciences are as true and steady as the needle to the pole, who will stand for the right if the heavens totter and the earth reels; men who can tell the truth, and look the world and the devil right in the eye; men who neither brag nor run; men who will neither flag or flinch;

men who have courage without shouting to keep it up; men in whom the current of everlasting life runs still, deep, and strong; men who will not fail nor be discouraged till judgment be set upon the earth; men who know their message and tell it; men who know their places and fill them; men who know their own business and mind it; men who will not lie; men who are not too lazy to work, nor too proud in order to be honest; men who are willing to care what they eat, and wear what they have paid for; and last, but not least—men who are willing "to do what they would that others should do unto them."

————

Give us Men!
Strong and stalwart ones;
Men whom highest hope inspires,
Men whom purest honor fires,
Men who trample Self beneath them,
Men who made their country wreath them
    As her noble sons,
Men who never shame their mothers,
Men who never fail their brothers
True, however false are others;
    Give us Men—I say again
    Give us Men!

Give us Men!
Men who, when the tempest gathers,
Grasp the standards of their fathers
    In the thickest fight;
Men who strike for home and altar,
(Let the coward cringe and falter)
    God defend the right;
True as truth, though lorn and lonely,
Tender, as the brave are only:
Men who tread where saints have trod,
Men for Country—Home—and God;
    Give us Men; I say again—again—
    Give us such Men!

                                        —Exeter

―――――

MEMORIES

The steam-powered passenger train of the 1930's had paused in Salt Lake City on a summery Monday morning. One of the passengers from the East stepped from the train to engage me in conversation:

"Will this train arrive in Los Angeles on time?" she asked.

"You're speaking of something more than seven hundred miles and about twenty-four hours away. But it should be on time."

"I'm traveling with my daughter. We thought we had plenty of time, but now I think her baby may come soon after we arrive in Los Angeles."

Together we stood and watched as the last canvas sack of the mountain of U.S. mail was placed in its car several cars ahead, and I said: "That's a good sign. We'll leave Salt Lake on time. Get back on the train."

An hour or so later I was helping the conductor with his recently collected tickets when she came by. "My daughter," she bit her lip. "Can you let us off at the next city?"

"This is the great west," the conductor answered. "There is no next city. We were hoping to find a doctor among the passengers when we took tickets, but we did not. We'll have to do our best for your daughter."

In a while there was a pitiful procession of a small group led by the Pullman Company maid to an unsold room accommodation on the train. The maid, the ill passenger, and the conductor went in and shut the door.

The older woman looked at the closed door, and then said to me: "Brakeman, there's nothing for me to do now but pray."

I went about the duties of seeing that the train was being properly operated. We were traveling sixty, but the stork caught up with us, and there was a baby's cry, and then the door opened with the conductor saying, "Come on in, Grandma, and meet your granddaughter."

In another moment he was saying: "Everything seems all right, doesn't it? Now, I'm no doctor. We'd like to put you off the train and into a hospital to make sure."

Several hours later as the train steamed into Milford an ambulance and a doctor was standing there, in response to our telegraphed message.

I helped the grandmother count their luggage as she said: "We'll never forget you and your kindness."

Thursday morning the conductor and I were standing watching a train come to a stop in Salt Lake City. It would be our train to take on toward Los Angeles.

"Good morning, Doctor," I said.

"Now cut that out. And if you see any women like that this morning, get them off right now. But I was quite relieved Tuesday in Milford to find a message from the doctor that after a night in the hospital, the mother, grandmother, and baby were in good condition."

Years went by—years that brought World War II and then the speed-up of passenger trains. Los Angeles became only about fifteen hours away—but still an overnight run.

One summery evening as we were leaving Salt Lake City the conductor called: "Tickets—have your tickets ready."

Halfway through the car an older woman exclaimed: "You're the ones. The very ones!" The eyes of the conductor's met mine. What had we done now? But if there was anything that the star (25 years service) and bars (5 years for each bar) on our uniform sleeve had taught us, it was to look wise and let a passenger fill in the details.

"Oh, how I've prayed that you'd be on this train. You brought my granddaughter here into the world at Jericho, Utah."

"Of course," we said, beating back the cobwebs in our memories.

"We named her Jericho. Jerrie, these are those wonderful men that we've often told you about.

When I found out that I could go to Los Angeles again, I wanted to bring Jerrie with me and show her the place where she was born."

"There's nothing much at Jericho any more," the conductor said.

"But we must see it."

At the appropriate time the conductor and I came for the woman and her granddaughter. As we walked through the train, I said: "Jerrie, your grandmother already knows that you're the best thing that ever happened at Jericho."

Then the two women, grandmother and teen-ager, were standing arm in arm at the best vantage point on the train.

"This is Jericho," the conductor said softly. And as if by signal the full moon came from behind a cloud to highlight the desolation of the place. We felt the big diesel engines up front strain and pull at the speeding train as if to leave that place in a hurry.

"Oh, Jerrie," the grandmother said, half aloud.

"Forgive an old woman; it is sometimes better to leave memories alone, to accept them only as we ourselves remember them."

—A. L. Zobell, Sr.

————

MIRACLES

A number of years ago Elder Francis M. Lyman [of the Council of the Twelve who was ordained an Apostle in 1880 and died in 1916 as president of that Quorum] and Elder B. H. Roberts [of the First Council of the Seventy who served in that Quorum from 1888 until he died in 1933 as its senior president] had attended a quarterly conference at Loa, Wayne County.

In those days traveling was by team and "white top." The brethren had started early that morning to catch the train fifty or sixty miles distant. They stopped for breakfast at Koosharem. While they were eating, a young man, seeing the "white top," knowing the elders were in the house, dismounted from his horse, entered and eagerly asked: "How long are you brethren going to stay here?"

"Just long enough to finish our breakfast. Why?" queried Elder Lyman.

"Because I should like to bring my uncle here and have you administer to him."

"If you can get him back here before we leave, we shall be glad to administer to him."

Before the brethren were through with their breakfast, there entered the living room of the house a man who was led in his physical blindness by his wife and this outstanding young rancher. As the elders entered the living room, Brother Lyman, in his big-hearted way, putting his hand on the man's knee, said: "Well, so you want to be administered to, do you?"

"No, I do not," was the surprising reply.

"Well, then," said President Lyman, "why are you here?"

"Because my wife and my nephew put me in the wagon and brought me here," was his frank statement.

"How long has it been since you lost your sight?" asked President Lyman. The man told him.

Brother Lyman said: "You believe the Lord can heal you, do you not?"

"Well, I think he can—I don't know if he will."

There seemed to be an absolute absence of faith so far as the man was concerned.

"Do you belong to the Church?" asked President Lyman.

"No, I do not," was the reply.

"If the Lord heals you, you would be glad to acknowledge his power should you not?"

"Yes, if he did, I think I should."

Let me tell you at this point now what seemed to me in that instance to be the most significant, and then I will finish the story. The young man had seen in a dream or vision the night before two men who had administered to his uncle and the latter had received his sight through that administration. That is what prompted him to dismount and make the request.

President Lyman and President Roberts performed the administration. The man, his wife, and nephew returned to their home. Presidents Lyman and Roberts resumed their journey to Salt Lake City.

Two or three months later, President Lyman was attending a conference in Blackfoot, Idaho. Among those who greeted him, walking unaided, was this man to whom they had administered.

"Do you remember me?" the man asked.

President Lyman said, "Yes, and I see you have received your sight."

"Yes, I have," said the man; "I can read a newspaper as well as you can."

During the brief interview that followed, President Lyman remarked: "I remember our conversation—how do you account for your having received your sight?"

"Well," said the skeptic, "I believe that the medicine I was taking had just begun to work."

There was the miracle, but its effect in converting the man to the power of God was nil.

To me a most important phase of the story is the pre-vision of that young rancher, for I know that pre-vision is an actual fact in life, and it was through his faith that the man had been blessed.

—President David O. McKay

MISSIONARIES

While on my first mission in the Eastern States I was asked:

"Why don't you 'Mormon' elders fly for higher game? Why do you always preach to the poor and lowly? Why don't you get up among the high and mighty? Take Henry Ward Beecher, for instance." (He was then alive, the great pastor of the Brooklyn Tabernacle.) "Convert him, and his whole congregation would flock in after him; and just see how that would build up your Church."

"That is not God's way of building up his Church," I replied. "The Lord declared by an ancient prophet, 'I will take you one of a city, and two of a family, and I will bring you to Zion: And I will give you pastors according to mine heart.'" (Jer. 3:14-15.)

I explained the great problem of the dispersion and gathering of Israel, whereby the blood of

Abraham, Isaac, and Jacob, the blood that believes, with spirits answering to that blood, who have been dispersed for a wise purpose among all nations, are now being recalled and brought together in a great movement called "the Gathering," preparatory to the building of the New Jerusalem and the glorious coming of the Lord.

And I added, "God is not anxious for great congregations. He is not desirous that any one person or people should make a bargain with him and join his Church as a business proposition."

—Elder Orson F. Whitney

————

My words are seldom strong, or bright,
    A woman's tones are low,
And 'tis not much a hand so slight
    Can offer thee, I know.
'Tis like the quivering breath that wakes
    When forest leaves are stirred,
Yet from a friend's true heart it takes
    To thee, a parting word,

Remember.

Remember—hope in thy sorrow,
    Remember—faith in thy prayer.

Remember—the bright tomorrow
    That dawns on the night's despair.
Remember—the hearts that love thee
    Are with thee—everywhere.
Remember—the path of duty
    When other paths seem fair.
Remember—the truth's white beauty
    When weak illusions glare.
And should the world defy thee
    Alone its strength to dare,
Remember, Heaven is nigh thee,
    Remember—God is there.

A friend's kind thoughts attend thy way
    Where e'er that way may be,
And so I make "remember"
    A parting word to thee.

                    —Miss S. E. Carmichael
            April 27, 1864, as John R. Young
            departed to fulfill an LDS mission
                in the Sandwich Islands (Hawaii)

———

The family was discussing the possibility of the son receiving a mission call.

"But," he said, "when I get through with my mission I'm going to do this and that."

"That may well be," the father replied, "but once you get the spirit of your call, you'll realize that real Latter-day Saints never quite get through with their missions and turn to something else."

MONEY

"Beware of how money is handled," cautioned an economics professor. "In fact, beware how the very word 'money' is used. A merchant once displayed a sign prominently proclaiming 'Money returned if not satisfactory.'

"One day a person came in and after stating a complaint about recently purchased merchandise, stated that he wanted his money back.

"And what was he told? You'd never guess. It was simply: 'We found that your money is entirely satisfactory and we therefore decline to return it.' "

MORTALITY

We have sometimes sat in awe, amazed by the mere numbers of people—each an expert in his own field—who are important enough to have their names listed at the end of a television program that we have particularly enjoyed.

And for every name that does appear, how many nameless people are also expending their time and talent to see that that particular program comes to the conclusion for which everything was planned?

Mortality is but a brief assignment in the eternities. We have wondered too, how long the list of people would be—teachers all, and each an expert in his field—to successfully bring an immortal spirit through mortal childhood, youth, maturity, and old age.

———

We have grasped the mystery of the atom and rejected the Sermon on the Mount. The world has achieved brilliance without wisdom, power without conscience. Ours is a world of nuclear giants and ethical infants. We know more about war than we know about peace, more about killing than we know about living.

—General Omar Bradley

———

MOTHERS

They were talking of the glory of the land beyond
    the skies,
Of the light and of the gladness to be found in
    paradise,
Of the flowers ever blooming, of the never-ceasing
    songs,
Of the wand'rings through the golden streets of
    happy, white-robed throngs;
And, said father, leaning cozily back in his easy
    chair,
(Father always was a master-hand for comfort
    everywhere):
"What a joyful thing 'twould be to know that
    when this life is o'er
One would straightway hear a welcome from the
    blessed, shining shore!"
And Isabel, our eldest girl, glanced upward from
    the reed
She was painting on a water jug, and murmured,
    "Yes, indeed."
And Marian, the next in age, a moment dropped
    her book,
And, "Yes, indeed!" repeated with a most ecstatic
    look;
But mother, gray-haired mother, who had come to
    sweep the room,
With a patient smile on her thin lips, leaned lightly
    on her broom—

Poor mother! no one ever thought how much she
    had to do—
And said: "I hope it is not wrong not to agree with
    you,
But seems to me that when I die, before I join the
    blest,
I'd like, just for a little while, to lie in my grave
    and rest."

—Anonymous

PIONEERS

All too frequently we think of pioneers in the
past tense. But there is still momentous pioneering
to be done out across tomorrow. Certainly there is
a challenge to the new generation of pioneers to
reassert the principles which have made us great
and which have kept us free.

Liberty can never be merely a mental concept.
It inheres in the spirit of people—it is born of
conscience and is sustained by emotional fervor
and by faith. Our churches can keep alive and stir
us with the spiritual ideals which guided the
fathers of our land. Those fathers knew that

religious liberty is bound up with economic and
political liberty.

—Elder Adam S. Bennion

———

Generally, when going out into the wild,
pioneers have been cheered and buoyed up by the
hopes before them, by the ties of affection,
binding them to friends left behind, by blessed
memories of friends and homes, and the knowledge that they will not be forgotten; but rather by
the wireless telegraphy of love, prayers will daily
and nightly ascend to heaven in their behalf.

But the exodus to Utah was not like any other
recorded in history. The exodus to Italy was to a
land of sunshine, native fruits, and flowers; the
march of "Zenophon's Immortal Band" was a
march of fighting men back to their homes; the
exodus of the Pilgrims was to a new world of
unmeasured possibilities; but the exodus to Utah
was a destination on the unresponsive breast of the
desert.

The Utah Pioneers had been tossed out of
civilization into the wilderness and on the outer
gate of that civilization a flaming sword of hate

had been placed, which was turned every way against the refugees.

All ties of the past had been sundered. They were so poor that their utmost hope was to secure the merest necessities of life. If ever a dream of anything like comfort or luxuries came to them, they made a grave in their hearts for that dream and buried it that it might no longer vex them.

Such was their condition as they took on their western march. The spectacle they presented was sorrowful enough to blind with tears the eyes of the angels of Pity and Mercy.

Day by day, the train toiled on its weary journey. There was the same limitless expanse of wilderness around them at dawn and at sunset. The same howl of wolves was their only lullaby as they sank to sleep at night. Only the planets and the far-off stars rolling on their sublime courses and smiling down upon them from the upper deep, were a nightly symbol that God still ruled, commanded order, and would not forget.

In sunshine and in storm they pressed onward for five hundred miles, then followed five hundred miles more over the rugged mountains which make the backbone of the continent. Their teams grew steadily weaker, more and more obstructions were interposed in their path, but they never faltered.

Men are supposed to bear such trials. These men had already received an experience which had, in a measure, prepared them for it. It was nothing for them to sleep with only the stars for a canopy. They had learned to economize food and clothing and to smile at hardships and fatigue. Again the toil of the day made a bed on the prairie seem soft as down when they sank to sleep. Moreover, they were not gifted with vivid imaginations; they had accepted a faith which made them patient and obedient, and one day was like another to them.

But what must the women of that company have endured? What longings must they have repressed, and smiled while repressing them? Women love gentle homes, they have innate desires for fair garments, rich adornments; they dream of surrounding their homes and those whom they love with grace and cheer and charm of their presence and accomplishments.

As the men slept, and the women lay listening to the bark of wolves and hoot of owls and they felt the wild around them peopled with uncanny things, what must have been the cross they bore?

They were nearing no land of vine and flowers and gold. Only the desert awaited them—the desert with its chill and its repellent face.

—Judge Charles C. Goodwin
a non-Mormon early Utah writer

———

PRAYER

A father had a new wristwatch and was showing it to his very young son. He took the boy by the hand and walked into a dark closet and the luminous dial glowed. In the dark the boy's eyes must have been as large as saucers, for he exclaimed:

"Show me how to turn it on, Daddy . . . let me turn it on, Daddy."

There was a great lesson there; a greater lesson for the father than for his son. In his secret place he recalled that the watch was with him always, but he realized that it was only turned on when the way was dark and unlighted.

Likewise, in his life he carried power, but that power was turned on—he hoped it was always on—only with the bend of the knees in frequent and honest prayer.

―――――

PREPARATION

During the great depression that characterized the early nineteen-thirties, Elder Adam S. Bennion, later a member of the Council of the Twelve, penned a series for the youth of the Church entitled "Facing Life." In one installment he discussed occupations and professions, concluding with this timeless thought:

"When you ask 'What fields are open?' the answer flashes back: 'Almost any field is open to you if you'll pay the price to get through the gate.' Can you dedicate yourself to that task in the spirit of Lincoln?

" 'I will study and prepare myself so that if the opportunity ever comes I shall be ready for it.' "

―――――

When the hour of action arises
The hour of preparation is past.

—Anonymous

―――――

PRIESTHOOD

In a discourse on priesthood at the October 1965 Semiannual General Conference of the Church, Elder William J. Critchlow, Jr., Assistant to the Council of the Twelve, said:

"Just as that great unseen electrical power flows through wires to bless mankind, so does that great unseen priesthood power flow through ordained men to bless mankind."

———

Someone has called the priesthood, "the Lord's fraternal organization."

———

RELIGION

"One would think," said a friend to Dr. Samuel Johnson, the celebrated man of letters, "that illness and the view of death would make men more religious."

"Sir," replied Johnson, "they do not know how to go about it. A man who has never had religion before, no more grows religious when he is ill, than a man who has never learned figures can count when he has need of calculation."

REPENTANCE

A boy walked into a house-painter's shop one day and stood looking at the different colors. The painter had gone out for something, and the boy thought he would investigate a little.

On the floor stood a keg containing thick white lead, and close beside it was a small can filled with bright red all ready for the brush. In each was a wooden paddle for stirring up the paint. The boy took hold of the paddle in the small can and held it up, watching the thin red stream which flowed from the end. Something startled him, and he turned quickly and let a single drop fall into the white lead. There it lay, one little red spot in the white mass.

The boy was frightened and wanted to repair the mischief which he had done, but he went at it the wrong way. The red paint had not mixed with the white, for the white was too stiff. If he had taken a little stick or the point of his pocket-knife, he might easily have lifted it out, and there would have been no harm really done.

Instead he tried to hide it by stirring it in. At first a little red streak followed the paddle round and round, soon it disappeared, but some of the lead was stained a very light pink. The boy stirred deeper and deeper, and at last he thought that the red streak was hidden, and it seemed to him that it was all clean and pure as ever.

But the first thing that the painter said when he came in and looked at it was, "This keg of white lead isn't very white. I wonder what's the matter with it?"

Some of us have tried to do the same thing with the spots on our lives that this boy did with the spot in the white paint. Instead of removing them, we seek to hide them. It's a very poor way. Root a sin out, and you are rid of it; leave it there, and no matter how well it is covered up, the painter will find it, if no one else does.

————

It would be of no use for a sinner to confess his sins to God, unless he were determined to forsake them; it would be of no benefit for him to feel sorry that he had done wrong unless he intended to do wrong no more; it would be folly for him to confess before God that he had injured his fellowman, unless he were determined to do all in his power to make restitution. Repentance, then, is not only a confession of sins, with a sorrowful, contrite heart, but a fixed, settled purpose to refrain from every evil way.

—Elder Orson Pratt

————

The principle of repentance is not peculiar to religion. Its equivalent exists in every human activity. The pattern is the same. When he learns better, the farmer no longer plants poor seed, the merchant no longer stocks goods not bought by the customers; the doctor lays aside old methods of treatment; the artist avoids paints that fade; and so on over the whole range of man's concerns. This is turning away from error.

There is a type of repentance in every industrial and scientific organization. If men want to succeed in any enterprise, they must practice repentance. Unless men laid aside poor methods for better ones, there would be no progress.

—Elder John A. Widtsoe

————

Today is the day of repentance. Someone has said that people who calculate on an eleventh hour repentance, generally die at 10:30.

—Elder John A. Widtsoe

———

One of the great musical instruments of the world is the Salt Lake Tabernacle Organ. Although it is not the largest in the world, it is one of the finest.

"There are many fine organs in the world," says Dr. Alexander Schreiner, chief Tabernacle Organist, "but which is the finest is a matter of taste. Organs are different, just as people are different. The Tabernacle Organ is outstanding, but this is partly because it is so well suited to the building in which it is housed. The Tabernacle, with its wooden floor and ceiling, acts as a huge wooden violin, which helps give the Organ its nobility of sound. This is something one cannot express; it must be felt. It is a matter of aesthetics."

The Organ has 189 ranks, with 10,846 pipes. About 2,000 of the pipes are wooden, about 100 of them from among the pipes in the original Tabernacle Organ of the late 1860's. In size, the pipes go all the way from those no larger than a child's little finger to the huge 32-foot wooden pipes that form a part of the ornamentation seen from the front. There are about 200 organ stops.

The Tabernacle Organ is daily being tuned, to keep it in top condition. (It takes about one month to go completely through the instrument.) At least two men are required for the task, with one at the keyboard of the console, the other inside. This area in back of the Organ is always kept remarkably clean, although few people see it. Often the Organ is tuned, even as it is being played on network broadcasts, as alert ears discover an offending note.

How like the story of the Organ is repentance! Man himself is the crowning point of creation. He is commanded to be clean, and to seek daily "tuning" with what he knows to be right. Then, even as he is going about his activities, he has the opportunity of correcting the very smallest things —the single notes—that may be amiss in his life.

RIGHTEOUSNESS

Nothing else is worth so much to you as your unqualified endorsement of yourself. The approval of the "still, small voice" within you, which says to every noble act, "That is right," and to every ignoble one "That is wrong," is worth more to you than all the kingdoms of the earth. It matters little what others may think about you, or what the world may say; it makes no difference whether the press or the public praises or blames; it is by your own honest judgment of yourself that you must stand or fall.

SABBATH

Brigham Young University was scheduled to play Loyola of Chicago on January 27, 1967, in a basketball tournament that was to feature many of the great university teams. The first day's games were cancelled as Chicago dug out of twenty-three inches of fresh fallen snow that drifted some places to fifteen feet deep.

Officials of the Chicago games reset the Friday (first-day) schedule for Sunday, but from the Provo, Utah, campus came word that the Cougars would not play on Sunday. Milton Hartvigsen, dean of the College of Physical Education, said: "It is not our policy to play athletic contests on Sunday, because we as Mormons observe that day as the Sabbath."

Saturday evening President Ernest L. Wilkinson of BYU, explaining the stand of the Church University, said: "We will not play on Sunday. We believe in athletics, but they do not supersede the Ten Commandments."

SERVICEMEN

During World War I a private sought promotion in the army. So often had he applied with unfavorable results that one day he went to his company commander determined to know the reason.

"I want to know why it is that I am constantly overlooked," he said, "while others are promoted over my head all the time."

"Do you really want to know?" the officer asked.

"Yes, sir, I do."

"Well, then, I'll tell you. You're a 'Mormon,' aren't you?"

"Yes, sir, I am, and I'm not ashamed of it!"

"I understand that your Church has a rule against the use of tobacco. Is that right?" the officer asked.

"Yes, sir, it is."

"Do you keep that rule?"

"No, sir, I don't because I—"

"Never mind the reason," the officer cut him short. "And your Church has another rule against gambling, hasn't it?"

"But I don't gamble, sir!"

"You do; because I saw you at it not a half-hour ago!" the officer corrected. "And another rule of your Church, I take it, is against lying—a rule which you also break, it seems. Qualities in an officer are courage and obedience to rules. You possess neither. If your parents and your Church haven't been able in twenty-one years to make a man out of you, Uncle Sam can't do it in two years. Good-bye."

———

On July 1, 1846, as the men—both young and old—departed to serve as volunteers in the Mor-

mon Battalion, this was the counsel given them by
President Brigham Young:

"Be humble, and pray every morning and
evening in your tents. A private soldier is as
honorable as an officer, if he behaves as well. . . .
Honor the calling of every man in his place. Keep
neat and clean, teach chastity, equality, and
civility; swearing must not be permitted. Insult no
man. Have no contentious conversations with any
class of people. Impose not your principles on any
people. Take your Bibles and Books of Mormon
with you; burn your cards, if you have any."

SIGN-SEEKING

When The Church of Jesus Christ of Latter-day
Saints was first founded, you could see persons
rise up and ask, "What sign will you show us that
we may be made to believe?"

I recollect a Campbellite preacher who came to
Joseph Smith, I think his name was Hayden. He
came in and made himself known to Joseph, and
said that he had come a considerable distance to
be convinced of the truth. "Why," said he, "Mr.
Smith, I want to know the truth, and when I am

convinced, I will spend all my talents and time in defending and spreading the doctrines of your religion, and I will give you to understand that to convince me is equivalent to convincing all my society, amounting to several hundreds."

Joseph commenced laying before him the coming forth of the work, and the first principles of the gospel, when Mr. Hayden exclaimed, "O, this is not the evidence I want, the evidence that I wish to have is a notable miracle; I want to see powerful manifestation of the power of God, I want to see a notable miracle performed; and if you perform such a one, then I will believe with all my heart and soul, and will exert all my power and all my extensive influence to convince others; and if you will not perform a miracle of this kind, then I am your worst enemy."

"Well," said Joseph, "what will you have done? Will you be struck blind, or dumb? Will you be paralyzed, or will you have one hand withered? Take your choice, choose which you please, and in the name of the Lord Jesus Christ it shall be done."

"That is not the kind of miracle I want," said the preacher.

"Then, sir," replied Joseph, "I can perform

none, I am not going to bring any trouble upon anybody else, sir, to convince you. I will tell you what you make me think of—the very first person who asked a sign of the Savior, for it is written in the New Testament, that Satan came to the Savior in the desert, when he was hungry with forty days' fasting, and said, 'If you be the Son of God, command these stones to be made bread.' Now," said Joseph, "the children of the devil and his servants have been asking for signs ever since; and when the people in that day continued asking him for signs to prove the truth of the gospel which he preached, the Savior replied, 'It is a wicked and an adulterous generation that seeketh a sign.' "

But the poor preacher had so much faith in the power of the Prophet that he daren't risk being struck blind, lame, dumb, or having one hand withered, or anything of the kind. We have frequently heard men calling for signs without knowing actually what they want. Could he not have tested the principles, and thus have ascertained the truth?

—President George A. Smith
Great Salt Lake City
June 24, 1855

SIN

The story is told that some shepherds once saw an eagle soar out from a crag. It flew majestically far up into the sky but by and by became unsteady and began to waver in its flight. At length one wing dropped and then the other, and the poor bird fell swiftly to the ground. The shepherds sought the fallen bird and found that a little serpent had fastened itself upon it while it was resting upon the crag.

The eagle did not know that the serpent was there, but it crawled through the feathers and while the proud monarch was sweeping through the air, its fangs were thrust into the eagle's flesh, and he came reeling into the dust.

This could be the story of many a life. Some secret sin has been eating its way into the heart, and at last a proud life lies soiled and dishonored in the dust.

————

The man who undertakes to live two lives will find that he is living but one, and that one is a life of deception.

Causes are true to their effect. That which you sow you will reap. If you live to the flesh, to the passions, to the corrupt inclinations, you may depend upon it that the fruit which is in store for you will be that which belongs to these things. There can be no doubt as to what your harvest will be.

If you think that after your day's business is done you can shut the blinds and carry on your orgies in secret with your evil companions; if you think you can serve the devil by night and go forth and look like a virtuous young man, that goes in the best society and does not drink, nor gamble, nor commit any vice, then the devil has his halter about your neck, and he leads you the stupid fool in all the crowd.

You deceive nobody but yourself. There is an expression in your eyes that tells stories. Passions strain clear through. A man might as well expect to take nitrate of silver—whose nature is to turn him a lead color—and not have the doctor know it, as to expect that he can form evil habits and pursue mischievous courses and not have it known.

It does not need a sheriff to search out and reveal the kind of life that you are living. Every law of God in nature is an officer after you. It does not require court, judge, and jury to try and condemn you.

All Nature is a courtroom, and every principle thereof is a part of that court which tries and condemns you.

Do not think that there can be such a monstrous misadjustment of affairs as that you can do the work of the devil and have the remuneration of an angel.

––––––––

SPEECH

When a man uses ten or fifteen superfluous words to convey one simple idea, his real meaning is lost, he reaches beyond all the rules of grammar and rhetoric, and his idea, which, had it been clothed with simple and appropriate language, might have been good, is lost for want of more suitable words. It is like Massa Gratian's wit—"two grains of wheat hid in three barrels of chaff."

—President George A. Smith

––––––––

Collecting his thoughts for the beginning of an address to the saints, January 3, 1858, Elder Orson Hyde said:

"I do not want my mind so trammelled as Brother Parley P. Pratt's once was, when dancing was first introduced into Nauvoo among the saints. I observed Brother Parley standing in the figure, and he was making no motion particularly, only up and down. Says I, 'Brother Parley, why don't you move forward?' Says he, 'When I think which way I am going, I forget the step; and when I think of the step, I forget which way to go.' "

———

Mark Twain and Chauncey M. DePew were both scheduled to appear on a program. Mr. Twain spoke for twenty minutes and made a big hit. When Mr. DePew was called on to speak, he said:

"Ladies and Gentlemen: Before this dinner Mark and I agreed to trade speeches. Mr. Twain just delivered my speech and I am pleased at the reception it has received. I regret that I have lost the notes to his speech and I can't remember what he wanted to say."

Mr. DePew then sat down amid much laughter, and was as big a hit as Mr. Twain.

That occasion is often recalled by a second speaker when a first speaker, accidentally or otherwise, has said everything that the second speaker had in mind.

————

"Be sure that they heard you say what you think they heard you say," was always the cheery farewell of a mission president to his missionaries.

————

SPIRITUALITY

Each one of us has in him a spirit and intelligence which, if we are to judge by the activities of our bodies, the carrying on of the work of our bodies, is far more intelligent than our conscious mind. Thus there appears to be, indeed it seems to me we are driven to declare that there is, a great wealth of intelligence which cannot be made available through certain super-mental or spiritual processes, the extent of their availability being wholly dependent upon the righteousness of our lives.

I can think of the problem in this way: an electric wire comes into your home, charged with enough electricity completely to light your whole house. Whether it does so or not depends upon how much of that current so delivered you are able to use. You can put upon that wire a thousand watt globe and get a thousand watt light, or you can put upon that wire a small globe and get a candle light. How much light you get depends upon how much resistance you throw into the circuit. The more resistance thrown in, the less light comes through.

As I see the matter, so is it with our intelligences. We have enough intelligence, enough spiritual current, completely to enlighten our souls. How much we get through depends upon the amount of resistance we throw into that circuit of spirit. Each coil of resistance thrown in, lessens by that much the light which comes out. Every evil thought and act is a resistance coil. If we keep constantly thinking evil thoughts, if we keep constantly doing evil deeds, we throw finally into the circuit so much resistance that little if any light can come through. This last is the condition of the man and the woman who fail to live in righteousness under the principles of the gospel; sin and iniquity obstruct the spiritual current from passing through.

–President J. Reuben Clark, Jr.

––––––––

SUCCESS

Charles F. "Boss" Kettering was the discoverer of many things about the motor car. He used to have a sign on his office wall in Detroit primarily for the benefit of his young aides and assistants. It read: "Do not bring me your successes, for they weaken me. Bring me your problems, for they strengthen me."

———

Here is a formula of truth: "When we fail to plan we plan to fail."

———

If you expect to accomplish anything in this world you must be alive—very much alive—alive all over. Some people seem half dormant. They impress you as partial possibilities—as people who have discovered only a small part of the continent within themselves. Most of it remains undeveloped territory.

A man who does things is one who is alive to the very tips of his fingers. He is alert, always on the watch for opportunities. He does not give idleness time to dissipate him. He fights against that common malady known as a "tired feeling" and conquers it.

Many a man is wondering why he does not succeed, while his desk, at which he sits, tells the story of his life, and shows the limitations of his capability. The scattered papers, the unfiled letters, the disorderly drawers, the layers of newspapers, of letters, of manuscripts, of pamphlets, of empty envelopes, of slips of paper, are all telltales.

If I were to hire someone, I would ask no better recommendation than would be afforded by the condition of his desk, or table, or room, or workbench, or counter, or books. We are all surrounded by telltales which are constantly proclaiming the stories of our lives, cover them up as we will. Our manner, our walk, our conversation, the glance of the eye, are all telling our life stories to the world.

We wonder why we do not get on faster, but these tiny biographers often tell the secret of our poverty, our limitations, our inferior positions.

———

TEMPTATION

I have heard a legend told of the Desert of Sahara.

There is a clump of trees situated in one of the most desolate spots in that great arid region. The roots of the trees are fed by hidden and undiscoverable springs, and in the shade of those trees the weary traveler is tempted to sit down and rest; and as he rests, the wind whistling through the leaves lulls him to sleep, and he dreams of home and its pleasures, and gradually he loses consciousness and his spirit takes its flight, his physical organism having been poisoned by the odor from the trees and the surrounding ground.

It looks as though mankind were in this condition. We are tempted by the plausible theories of men to pay a little for our religion, and thus be lulled to sleep, picturing in our imaginations the beauties of eternity, until we gradually pass away from this life and find that our sleep has been the sleep of death—eternal death, because we have neglected the opportunities which God has placed in our way for our exaltation.

—Elder Abraham H. Cannon

If I were to ask you today, what would you take for your standing and your privileges as Latter-day Saints, is there anything that you could name? There is nothing. You would say, if the wealth of the world were to be laid at your feet in exchange, you would spurn it as a thing of naught.

But Satan does not tempt us in that style; he knows better.

If a man who was in the enjoyment of the Spirit of God one year ago had been told that yesterday, the seventh of October, a trifling temptation would be presented to him of a certain character (and that at the time he would think contemptible), and he would yield to it, he would be astonished, he would scarcely believe it.

"What! will I barter the wealth that God has given me, the wealth of the gospel, the wealth of freedom which is contained in it! What! will I barter the joy, peace, and happiness which I now have for so contemptible a temptation as that? Will I do it? No; I will not."

Yet the year passes away, and the seventh of October comes to hand, the temptation is presented, and the man who thought himself so impregnable in the truth, and thought that he could not be tempted and seduced from it, falls a victim, and to what? to the wealth of the world? No; but to something that is so truly contemptible, mean, and low, that it is a matter of astonishment to everybody who knows him how he could be overcome by it.

—President George Q. Cannon

TESTIMONY

Sometimes men say, "I have a testimony of the gospel." I believe them. Sometimes I hear them say, "I know the gospel is true," and I believe them. But especially with missionaries I have said time and again in various mission fields:

"When I hear you say, 'I know the gospel is true,' I would like to stop you and have you repeat that but say only, 'I know the gospel.'"

Of course it is true if it is the gospel, but do you know the gospel?

—President Hugh B. Brown

———

Some years ago, a leading educator of our country who was attending the National Education Association in Salt Lake City was taken by the writer up one of our canyons. On the way this educator began to ask questions about the organization of the Church. He was given a rather complete explanation of the religious system with its various quorums of the priesthood and its different auxiliary organizations.

After a few moments of silence, the educator remarked: "That is the most wonderful organization I have ever known. Why," he added with earnestness, "if we had that system everywhere we could revolutionize the world."

"I am not quite sure you could," returned this writer.

"Why not?"

"Simply because everyone would not accept with this system the one thing that gives it force and power for good."

"What do you mean?" he inquired.

It happened we were passing at the moment an electric power plant which stood at the mouth of the canyon.

"Let me make my answer to your question clearer by an analogy. You see that electric plant. Now let us suppose such a plant was built with its pipe lines, its turbines, its poles and wires, its transformers, its lamps and other essential equipment. Suppose also that there was no water power available to turn into the pipes. What would be the use of all of your electric system?"

"It would be useless of course," he returned, "but how does this analogy apply to the question at issue?"

"Right here: The inner strength of Mormonism comes from the free will service of its members in the cause. It offers to each and all opportunity to serve without other reward than that which comes to them in the form of increase of their talents and in spiritual self-development. Would people generally be ready to give their time and talents—to take on responsible positions in the Church, to sing in the choir, to go on missions, and otherwise to devote their lives in generous measure without thought of pay, with only love of the work of the Master?"

"I am afraid not," he replied.

"Then what would be the use of the organization I have explained?"

"What puzzles me," he responded, "is, How can you get people to do all this work without monetary compensation?"

"The reason is simple," I replied. "They believe in the divinity of the work."

—Elder Howard R. Driggs

TESTING

Let us all take a course to do right, and, if we all do right, there is no person here that will do wrong. I am aware that there will have to be a sifting, but would there be any necessity for it if the elements were pure? No. You can obtain pure sand here upon the public works, and with that you can make good tempered mortar, for the better it is tempered the better wall you can put up for your habitation. Temper the mortar and let the sand be clear of stone, roots, and every imperfect thing.

If this were the case the masons would have no use for the coarse screen to throw the sand against, nor for a fine sieve to separate the finer particles. It is just so with us. The Lord will keep sifting, and will prepare a riddle and sieve, that is, the devil will riddle you, and after that he will sift you. Did not the Savior tell one of his disciples that the devil desired to sift him as wheat is sifted?

–President Heber C. Kimball
September 19, 1852

TODAY

Yesterday is gone forever. Tomorrow never comes. Today is in my own hands.

If I shirk Today's task, I shall be adding to wasted Yesterdays.

If I postpone Today's duty, I shall be increasing Tomorrow's burdens.

If I accomplish what Today sets before me, I shall be doing my best to atone for Yesterday's failures, and to prepare for Tomorrow's successes.

Therefore, I will endeavor so to use my time and opportunities that Today shall leave me a little wiser and abler than it found me.

———

After the battles of Okinawa in World War II the Americans buried their dead in a cemetery that bore the inscription, "We gave our todays in order that you might have your tomorrows."

———

Charles Dickens laid this setting for his book, *A Tale of Two Cities:*

"It was the best of times, it was the worst of times; it was the age of wisdom, it was the age of foolishness; it was the epoch of belief, it was the

epoch of incredulity; it was the season of light, it
was the season of darkness; it was the spring of
hope, it was the winter of despair; we had
everything before us, we had nothing before
us. . . ."

————

Some skies may be gloomy,
    Some moments be sad;
But everywhere, always,
    Some souls must be glad;
For true to the saying,
    Proclaimed by the seer—
"Each day is the best day
    Of somebody's year!"

Each day finds a hero,
    Each day helps a saint,
Each day brings to some one
    A joy without taint;
Though it may not be my turn
    Or yours that is near—
"Each day is the best day
    Of somebody's year!"

The calendar sparkles
    With days that have brought
Some prize that we hoped for,
    Some good that we sought;

High deeds happen daily,
   Wide truths grow more clear—
"Each day is the best day
   Of somebody's year!"

No sun ever rises
   But brings joy behind,
No sorrow in fetters
   The whole earth can bind;
How selfish our fretting,
   How narrow our fear—
"Each day is the best day
   Of somebody's year!"

—Youth's Companion

TROUBLES

A man had built a service-pit in the lean-to that served as his garage and workshop. The family knew it was there and never considered it to be hazardous. Each of them had driven the family car in and out of its place literally hundreds of times. But one day as his wife started home from her errand in the car she thought of that service-pit. As she continued to think, she thought of all the hazards of it, and fear gripped her. Not being able to shake the fear, she stopped the car as she drove in, got out and pushed the car into its accustomed place over the service-pit! The fear of not what happened but what could happen had become her master.

———

Have you noticed how shore birds and gulls face into the wind when they are at rest on the beach? Of course—it keeps their feathers in perfect position. A good philosophy is to face your troubles; don't let them ruffle your feathers.

———

UNDERSTANDING

If you cannot on the ocean
   Sail among the swiftest fleet,
Rocking on the highest billows,
   Laughing at the storms you meet;
You can stand among the sailors
   Anchored yet within the bay,
You can lend a hand to help them
   As they launch their boats away.

If you are too weak to journey
   Up the mountain steep and high,
You can stand within the valley
   While the multitudes go by;

You can chant in happy measure
    As they slowly pass along;
Tho' they may forget the singer,
    They will not forget the song.

If you have not gold and silver
    Ever ready to command,
If you cannot to the needy
    Reach an ever-open hand;
You can visit the afflicted,
    O'er the erring you can weep,
You can be a true disciple,
    Sitting at the Savior's feet.

If you cannot in the conflict
    Prove yourself a soldier true,
If, where fire and smoke are thickest,
    There's no work for you to do;
When the battlefield is silent,
    You can go with careful tread,
You can bear away the wounded,
    You can cover up the dead.

Do not, then, stand idly waiting
    For some greater work to do;
Fortune is a lazy goddess—
    She will never come to you;

Go and toil in any vineyard,
  Do not fear to do or dare,
If you want a field of labor
  You can find it anywhere.

—Anonymous

————

Blindfolded and alone I stand,
With unknown thresholds on each hand;
The darkness deepens as I grope,
Afraid to fear, afraid to hope;
Yet the one thing I learn to know
Each day more slowly as I go,
That doors are opened, ways are made,
Burdens are lifted or are laid
By some grand law unseen and still,
Unfathomed purpose to fulfill—
  "Not as I will."

Blindfolded and alone I wait;
Loss seems too bitter, gain too late;
Too heavy burdens in the load,
And too few helpers on the road;
And joy is weak and grief is strong,
And years and days so long, so long!

Yet this one thing I learn to know
Each day more surely as I go,
That I am glad the good and ill
By changeless law are ordered still—
   "Not as I will."

"Not as I will," the sound grows sweet
Each time my lips the words repeat;
"Not as I will," the darkness feels
More safe than light when this thought steals
Like whispered voice to calm and bless
All unrest and all loneliness.
"Not as I will," because the One
Who loved us first and best has gone
Before us on the road, and still
For us must all his love fulfill—
   "Not as we will?"

                              —Helen Hunt Jackson

                    ————————

VALUES

The dedication of a man's life to the kingdom of God does not mean the abridgment of opportunity, the surrender of righteous interests or the inhibition of any experience that will contribute to his permanent peace and happiness. On the contrary it means subscribing to the eternal principles of progress and growth; it means pursuing the path that leads to self-mastery, exaltation and glory; it means availing one's self of that divine assistance which comes from above, and which is promised to all who accept the truth and covenant in baptism to serve God and obey his word. In other words, to follow this admonition is to live abundantly, to build the noblest and grandest character possible—that is the paramount object of life.

A man may accumulate a fortune but, be it ever so great, if in the process he loses his own soul he is "in the light of eternity" indeed poor.

A man may write a book, build a skyscraper, make discoveries, distinguish himself in the field of politics and statesmanship, but if he loses his own soul doing it he sustains an irreparable loss, for "what profiteth a man though he gain the whole world and lose his own soul?"

To measure and equate life's values wisely is indeed the highest wisdom. It means success here and hereafter.

What am I?

No one has a good word for me, but I am tolerated everywhere. I am found in the palaces of the rich and in the hovels of the poor. I am thoroughly evil, but I have adherents even among the righteous.

I cause hunger and want and open the way for pestilence and famine. I benefit no one, and injure all with whom I come in contact. I thrive in the indifference, ignorance, and apathy of the people.

Because of me nations topple and fall. I am the partner and associate of political corruption and decay. In time of war I undermine defense and cause battles to be lost.

I sap the life blood of the nation and leave her open to despoilers. Though I handicap and hinder the valiant defenders of the nation, there is no uprising against me. I am a traitor and saboteur, but I am found in every department of government.

I take much and give nothing of value in return. I consume and destroy the fruits of the industrious and degrade the poor. I lower the standard of living, for I reduce production. I cause contempt for the law because of my prevalence in government.

I weaken and injure mankind, but strangely, it does not vigorously and increasingly fight me. Now I should, and could be destroyed, but I thrive as never before. I am an enemy of civilization.

What am I?

I am waste—waste of manpower, waste of substance, waste of life, waste of time.

———

A cobbler sang from morn till night:
'Tis sweet and marvelous to hear;
His trills and quavers told the ear
Of more contentment and delight,
Enjoyed by that laborious wight,
Than e'er enjoyed the sages seven,
Or any mortals short of heaven.

His neighbor, on the other hand,
With gold in plenty at command,
But little sang, and slumbered less—
A financier of great success.

If e'er he dozed at break of day,
The cobbler's song drove sleep away;
And much he wished that Heaven had made
Sleep a commodity of trade,
In market sold, like food and drink,
So much an hour, so much a wink.

At last, our songster did he call
To meet him in his princely hall.
Said he, "Now, honest Gregory,
What may your yearly earnings be?"

"My yearly earnings! faith, good sir,
I never reckon in that way,"
The cheerful cobbler said,
And queerly scratched his head—
"I never reckon in that way.
But cobble on from day to day,
Content with daily bread."

"Indeed! Well, Gregory, pray,
What may your earnings be per day?"
"Why sometimes more and sometimes less.
The worst of all, I must confess,
(And but for which our gains would be
A pretty sight indeed to see)
In that the days are made so many
In which we cannot earn a penny.
The sorest ill the poor man feels:
They tread upon each other's heels.
Those idle days of holy saints!
And though the year is shingled o'er,
The parson keeps a-finding more!"
With smiles provoked by these complaints,

Replied the lordly financier,
"I'll give you better cause to sing.
Three hundred pounds I hand you here
Will make you happy as a king.
Go, spend them with a frugal heed:
They'll long supply your every need."

The cobbler thought the silver more
Than he had ever dreamed, before,
The mines for ages could produce,
Or world with all its people use.
He took it home, and there did hide
And with it laid his joy aside.

But cares, suspicions, in their stead,
And false alarms, by fancy fed.
His eyes and ears their vigils keep,
And not a cat can tread the floor
But seems a thief slipped through the door.

At last, the poor, bewildered man
Up to the financier he ran—
Then in his morning nap profound:
"Oh, give me back my songs," cried he.
"And sleep, that used so sweet to be,
And take the money, every pound!"

—Jean De La Fontaine
(Translated by Elizur Wright)

WISDOM

Every man is the builder of a temple, called his body, to the God he worships, after a style purely his own, nor can he get off hammering marble instead. We are all sculptors and painters and our material is our own flesh and bones. Any nobleness begins at once to refine a man's features; any meanness or sensuality, to imbrute them.

—Henry D. Thoreau

———

These "terse sayings" from the writings of Henry D. Thoreau:

. . . Superfluous wealth can buy superfluities only.

. . . Only the day dawns to which we are awake.

. . . My friend is that one whom I can associate with my choicest thoughts.

. . . To enjoy a thing exclusively is commonly to exclude yourself from the true enjoyment of it.

. . . What a fool he must be to think his El Dorado is anywhere but where he lives.

. . . A grain of gold will gild a great surface, but not so much as a grain of wisdom.

. . . A man is rich in proportion to the number of things he can afford to let alone.

. . . If you build castles in the air, your work need not be lost; that is where they should be. Now put the foundations under them.

. . . Life is grand and so are its environments of Past and Future. Would the face of nature be so serene and beautiful if man's destiny was not equally so?

. . . All men want, not something to do with, but something to do, or rather, something to be.

WORD OF WISDOM

"It is certainly surprising," said a grocer, "just how many people come by my checkstand complaining bitterly at the price of a loaf of bread that they are buying—it has gone up a cent—and then they say casually: 'Oh, I need three packs of cigarettes.' And they never question the price of those things."

Once I was driving along and had two young men with me in my car and a young man thumbed a ride with us. I asked the boys that were with me if we should take him with us and they said yes.

I picked him up, and after we had driven along a little way he said, "Do you mind if I smoke in your car?"

I said, "No, not at all, if you can give me any good reason why you should smoke." And I said, "I will go farther than that." (I was a stake president at this time.) "If you can give me a good reason why you should smoke, I will smoke with you."

Well, these two young men looked at me and wondered. We drove on for some distance, about twenty minutes, I think, and I turned and said:

"Aren't you going to smoke?"

And he said, "No."

I said, "Why not?"

"I can't think of a good reason why I should."

I would like that word to go to all of our young

men, and when you can think of a good reason,
and only when you can, then begin to smoke.

—President N. Eldon Tanner

WORK

Over a well-worn work bench once hung these
words: "If you haven't the time to do it right the
first time, when are you going to have the time to
do it over?"

Paderewski, the genius at the concert piano of
another age, rented rooms in order to practice
unmolested. A friend, hearing of this, thought it
would be a good opportunity to learn from the
master's practice hours, so he rented rooms direct-
ly above. The first day of practice, Paderewski
played the same passage over about five hundred
times. The friend paid the rent on the room and
left.

But it is this dogged, critical repetition which
makes great men and women in all the walks of
life. Make every day's practice successful, no
matter how little the success may be at the

moment. The way to reach the ideal tomorrow is to make today a day of work instead of a day of hope. Work, and do not worry.

———

Without faith and enterprise, nothing is begun; without patience and perseverance, nothing is finished.

———

YOUTH

Later life is largely the working out of the visions and the enthusiasms which come to us in youth. For youth is not only the beginning, but the perennial spring, of all our faculties.

The real test of the man is not, How much skill has he? but, How much youth abides in his soul?

Whether the long stretches of middle life, under the heat of the sun and the burden of the day, shall be a monotonous and barren plain, or blossom as a garden continually freshened by crystal waters, depends upon the depth and volume of the springs of youth.

There are men of few years but great age. We have all seen them—those old men of thirty or forty, who have fingered the fringe of life with the tips of their idle hands, and imagine they are sated, worn-out men of the world. They have exhausted, as they believe, all of life's resources, and for them the years hold nothing but monotony and weariness. Nonentities.

And we have seen those other men on whose strong, trained shoulders rest the burdens of seven, eight, and sometimes nine decades, full of the unwasted power of the spirit, electric with energy, virile with that strength which comes of freshness and of joy in the work done and the vision fulfilled.

Life is measured not by its years, but by its enthusiasms.

While the vision glows, the life is young. Only when the vision fades is the life here done.

———

Young people are born as good as ever. They still dream of happy lives. They hope for success. They would rather be good than bad. But, times have changed. There are gilded temptations today that were unknown yesterday. There are enticing opportunities, bearing the stolen badge of freedom, which were not permissible in earlier days. Youth, themselves, in this dangerous age, need to seek protection against temptation. If trained right, they should more than ever cooperate with parents in establishing worthy homes. The commandment to "Honor thy father and thy mother: that thy days may be long upon the land . . ." (Exodus 20:12) remains in full force. They should abide, gladly, by the law of God and man, which leaves children subject to their parents until maturity arrives. Above all, they should make conformity with God's law their chief desire. Youth should keep in mind that the path to success is paved with self-control.

—Elder John A. Widtsoe